P9-CCO-191

LEE COUNTY LIBRARY
107 Hawkins Ave.
Sanford, NC 27330

PRESS ON!

PRESS ON!

Further Adventures in the Good Life

BY

GENERAL CHUCK YEAGER
&
CHARLES LEERHSEN

LEE COUNTY LIBRARY
107 Hawkins Ave.
Sanford, NC 27330

BANTAM BOOKS
TORONTO • NEW YORK • LONDON • SYDNEY • AUCKLAND

PRESS ON!

A Bantam Book / October 1988

Grateful acknowledgment is made to General Chuck Yeager and to Clarence E. "Bud" Anderson for use of the photographs in this book.

All rights reserved.
Copyright © 1988 by Yeager Family Partnership, Ltd.,
Donald Yeager, Michael D. Yeager, Sharon C. Yeager Flick,
and Susan Finnegan Yeager.
No part of this book may be reproduced or transmitted
in any form or by any means, electronic or mechanical,
including photocopying, recording, or by any information
storage and retrieval system, without permission in
writing from the publisher.
For information address: Bantam Books.

Library of Congress Cataloging-in-Publication Data

Yeager, Chuck, 1923–
Press on!

  1. Yeager, Chuck, 1923–   . 2. Test pilots—
United States—Biography. I. Leerhsen, Charles.
II. Title
TL540.Y4A3   1988   623.74'6048'0924   [B]   88-16690
ISBN 0-553-05333-7

Published simultaneously in the United States and Canada

Bantam Books are published by Bantam Books, a division of
Bantam Doubleday Dell Publishing Group, Inc. Its trademark,
consisting of the words "Bantam Books" and the portrayal of a
rooster, is Registered in U.S. Patent and Trademark Office and
in other countries. Marca Registrada. Bantam Books, 666 Fifth
Avenue, New York, New York 10103.

PRINTED IN THE UNITED STATES OF AMERICA

DH   0   9   8   7   6   5   4   3   2   1

CONTENTS

ACKNOWLEDGMENTS

The authors are grateful for the help they received in the form of comments and recollections from Mr. and Mrs. Dell Riebe, Hal Yeager, Jr., Pansy Lee Yeager, Susie Yeager Finnegan, Victor Belenko, Mr. and Mrs. Ed Bowlin, and Cindy Siegfried. Ian Ballantine deserves special thanks for conceiving the project and overseeing it until it reached the stage where Betty Ballantine's deft editing came into play. Clarence "Bud" Anderson, in particular, gave freely of his time and energy, both in offering reminiscences and to check important details throughout the manuscript. And finally, Glennis Yeager, most especially, provided insight, opinion, anecdotes, access to the General's current life-style, and inspiration.

1

SUMMER, AND
SO THE SIERRAS

As a barefoot kid in bib over-
alls, I used to wander the West Virginia woods for countless hours, always wanting to see what was around the
next bend, beyond a big boulder, over the next rise. My
feet were so callused they were tougher than any shoes. I
don't think I was looking for anything in particular on
those day-long jaunts; I was just an incredibly curious kid
with a vague notion that one of these days I'd discover
some grand, new wonder, maybe a place that would be
some kind of Shangri-la, where the trees and rocks and
the water formed a scene more beautiful than anyplace
else on earth. It was a childish fantasy and I eventually
forgot about it—until the day, very much later, after I'd
returned from the War and was living far from the fields
and mountains of my home state, when I finally found
that special place that I'd been searching for.

I was so excited, I think I actually let out a whoop when
I first saw that promised land from the air.

I'm talking about the Sierra Nevada Mountains.

The Sierras—whose name in Spanish means "snowy

1

sawtoothed range"—is a spectacular series of high peaks and deep dramatic valleys that extends for 430 miles in the eastern part of California, from the Feather River south to the Tehachapi Pass. It's impossible to generalize about the area, because it includes lush meadows, high waterfalls, sheer cliffs, and lakes more than 1000 feet deep. For my money, though, it's the most beautiful place on the planet.

My annual trip into the Sierras is now the central event in my life. I may go salmon fishing in Alaska, fly casting for trout in Scotland, deer hunting in Marfa, Texas, or boar hunting in Germany. Or I may not. But the Sierra trip is sacred; it goes off like clockwork each summer no matter what. I take no commitments during the first two weeks in July, despite tremendous pressure to be in some parade or other gaudy event on the Fourth. Even if the President of the United States calls, my wife, Glennis, knows to politely inform him that I'm making my annual backpacking trip with my best friend, Andy, my brother, Hal, and maybe one or two other friends.

And once the trip starts there's just no way to interrupt it. While I'm up there scrambling over rocks and crunching around on big patches of leftover winter snow, there is virtually no way of reaching me. It is fourteen days or so completely cut off from newspapers, television, and radio, and it is exhilarating to be so totally out of touch that you are left with only the mountains and your own thoughts.

The Sierras is where I feel most alive.

They say you form your strongest attachment to the places and people you encounter in childhood, but for me that hasn't been true. By the time I discovered the Sierras I wasn't a naive kid anymore but a twenty-two-year-old captain with a record as a double ace in World War II,

2

a young wife, and two young sons, Donald and Mickey. I had been halfway around the world from my hometown in Hamlin. I'd walked the streets of blacked-out, war-torn London, flown through the skies above Nazi Germany, and hidden out in the forests of occupied France. In other words, I was a certified adult. And yet I still had enough of my boyhood curiosity so that practically the first thing I did when I arrived in 1945 at Muroc Army Air Field (later renamed Edwards Air Force Base) for early tests on jets was to grab a plane and check the area out.

I'd seen the Alps and the Pyrenees from the air, and I'd watched the sun come up on the Atlantic Ocean—but I was truly taken aback by the spectacular beauty of the Sierras, stretching away for several hundred miles to the north of where I'd be working. I remember kind of whistling through my teeth and thinking, "Wait till Andy sees all this."

I guess I'd finally found the Shangri-la I'd been looking for. Dropping down to an altitude of 12,000 feet, I could see huge gray-white granite-walled canyons and lakes as pure as the snow that ran down from the blazing white peaks and kept the waterways constantly replenished.

Those lakes would be brimming, I suspected, with golden trout. The golden, which is the state fish of California, can be found only at elevations of 9000 feet and above. Not only are they handsome to look at and a challenge to catch, those gold and red beauties are known, quite deservedly, as one of the most delicious fish in America. You can't get that delicate pink meat in even the finest restaurants, though, since it would not make economic sense to pack them out of the mountains. No, the only way to experience a golden legally is to grab your spinning or flycasting gear and hike high up in those mountains. Then, if you're lucky (or smart) enough to catch some, you can cook them up over a crackling fire, pull a few wild onions out of the ground as a side dish—and that's a meal that's really got "The Right Stuff."

(A footnote on that famous phrase: even years after that book was written I am still asked continually if I have "the right stuff"—and I am still explaining to people that I don't know what the hell that means. Tom Wolfe, the author, invented it and made a lot of money off it, but it's not something I've ever heard any pilot say. A nice guy, Tom, we run into each other occasionally on the speaking circuit, but I've never understood a lot of what he was driving at. Once, a few years ago, he sent me a bunch of his books to read, but I never got past the titles, they were so weird. "Velvet Gloves and Mauve Something" was one, I think. I prefer Louis L'Amour any day. Louis, whom I used to see each summer at the American Academy of Achievement, wrote in a simple, straightforward style about black hats and white hats, and that's a world I can identify with.)

One of the things that fascinated me from the start about the Sierras was how different they were from my old stomping grounds in West Virginia. Tooling around up there in the Pacific-blue sky, I could see an infinite number of foxtail and lodgepole pines, but no beeches or any other kinds of trees we had back home. On the lower elevations the Sierra pine forests grew lushly, but at the timberline the relatively few trees that survived in the thin air twisted themselves, as they grew, into spectacular specimens that looked like modern sculpture.

From the air looking down, I felt like a kid with my nose pressed up against the toy store window. But I knew that just seeing this countryside wasn't going to be enough. I wanted to run my hands along the knotted and gnarled

4

trunks of those thousand-year-old pines and feel wood so dense that it would be as hard and as sharp as solid jade. I wanted to fish those clear-as-crystal lakes, and walk the trails and face the challenges of that unspoiled land, whatever they might be. Just looking at it, I knew I could never cover every acre of that magnificent wilderness. Realizing that made me feel that I was, in a sense, "set for life" and wealthy beyond my wildest dreams.

I've never smoked or chewed tobacco, and I gave up alcohol without a second thought a number of years ago— the only thing I'm addicted to is adrenaline. The Sierras got my adrenaline flowing like nothing else since the War—and what a relief that was. I had seriously wondered if my combat experience hadn't been an impossibly tough act to follow, if perhaps the rest of my life was going to be one long letdown. But in 1945 I had a new career as a test pilot at Muroc, and those mountains to explore. Both gave me fresh challenges that might very well have been my salvation.

As it turned out, both the flying and the hiking exceeded my expectations. Those two aspects of my life also complemented each other. By the time Friday night rolled around, I was really ready to let off some steam. Hunting and fishing, for me, have always been a form of recreation. Even if I don't get a bird, fish, or a deer, it's no big disappointment as long as I get the exercise and the chance to breathe some fresh air, hear that special brand of "Sierra silence," and watch the sunrise.

My feeling for the Sierras is something I share with my friend Andy. His name is Clarence Emil "Bud" Anderson, but to me he's always been Andy. We met early on, before the War, when I was still in training. Both of us were right around nineteen, although Andy had a year on me. We got shipped out together, went through the War together, and our lives have been closely linked ever since. I've probably shared more experiences with Andy than with anybody in my life except Glennis.

Of course, in the old days we thought of recreation as kind of a gung-ho macho thing that had little to do with fitness and health. Most of the time I'd begin my weekends in the wilderness by heading to the officers' club, where I'd have a few belts with the boys. Then we'd go home and grab our fishing rods or rifles and head off—if not deep into the Sierras, then at least into the foothills to have the kind of fun that perhaps only test pilots who put their asses on the line for a living could readily understand.

I can remember one time back in 1948 when we took off from Edwards one Friday night, determined to celebrate the fact that we'd survived another week without drilling a deep hole in the California desert. We were headed for a good fishing spot up by Crowley Lake in California, a good three-hour drive under the best of circumstances— which these were not.

Our transportation that night was a '39 Chevrolet sedan that was being held together by a buddy of ours named John Thornberry. John was a "tech rep," which means he was a civilian assigned to advise the Air Force on a particular piece of equipment that his company had sold to the military. Good thing he was mechanically inclined, too, because that old car of his had a worn-out vacuum shift, and every time he'd move it into second gear and let the clutch out, we'd hear this *boing, boing, boing* noise and we'd have to stop.

"No problem, no problem," John would say. Well, maybe. But one of us would always have to roll up his sleeves, get down under the hood, and do the dirty work of realigning the shift-forks.

Of course, the *reason* John kept having to shift into

second so much was that he'd see a bar coming up in one of those whistle-stop western towns that lay between Edwards and our fishing spot and wanted to check each one out. So each time the car broke down, we'd all have ourselves a stiff drink.

After about eight or ten of these pit stops we were pretty greased up, inside and out. That poor Chevy, meanwhile, was throwing off pieces of itself like there was no tomorrow. Finally, we coasted to a halt that was somehow different from all the previous breakdowns. I just knew that no amount of fiddling and farting around could make that car go on.

Normal people would no doubt have abandoned all hope of continuing on any kind of excursion into the outdoors at this point. But not us; we were going to get in our weekend of fishing and hunting and hell-raising if it killed us. So while the other four or five guys stayed with the car, I hitched a ride back to the town of Mojave and called Glennis, who arranged for a couple of air policemen from the base to meet us in my car.

It was not strictly in accordance with the rules to have enlisted men help us with our fishing trip, but what the hell. I've always said that the rules are made for people who aren't willing to make up their own—and, as far as I was concerned, that never described me and my friends.

In any case, by the time the air policemen arrived to give us a hitch, it got to be awfully late; in fact, it was daybreak Saturday morning before we finally got to Crowley Lake. We were hung over and dog tired. But we were used to adversity, so we immediately threw our packs on our backs and headed off into the woods.

John Thornberry was neither military nor as driven to fish and hunt as we were. From the moment we started out I could see he was stepping through the woods with that special kind of care that an excess of alcohol induces in some people. Then halfway across this footbridge, which spanned a gorge with a pretty good-size creek swirling down below, he made the mistake of remembering that he was only half sober and dazed from fatigue. And so he panicked. Which in this case meant that he laid down right on his face and hugged that log for dear life while the rest of us stood around, roaring with laughter and cheering him on. After a good seven or eight minutes he finally started inching his way across like some goddamn caterpillar, which sent us all into new fits of laughter. It really was very funny.

A good guy, John Thornberry, but what he did wrong in that situation was to stop and imagine a worse-case scenario. And so he froze up. It's like that with a lot of things in life. Often, the possibilities are frightening, but what good does it do to stop in your tracks and start fretting? When the going gets tough, just about all you can do is keep going forward, and press on as determinedly as you can.

OTHER VOICES

Bud Anderson

Chuck always had a way of going all-out in everything he did. His jokes were usually on the rough side, and he's never had too many stressful moments worrying about other people's feelings.

That may sound a little cruel, but the fact is that if Chuck didn't think highly of someone on some level, he would never bother with him in the first place. A potential hiking buddy doesn't have to know a lick about airplanes or fishing or any of the things that Chuck is interested in. But if someone is, as Chuck says, "clever" at something—being a salesman, an administrator, or anything—Yeager immediately respects him for that and figures he's the kind of guy we can have some fun with. In other words, someone who is really good at doing whatever it is he does is likely to be someone who can also take a joke.

I've had every kind of experience imaginable in the Sierras. I remember one trip, back in the fifties, when we were up near the south fork of the San Joaquin River. The days were filled with the beautiful rainbows so common up there, but during the nights we kept hearing the sound of dogs howling.

If we hadn't run out of booze several days before, I'd have thought I was hearing things. In fact, the idea of encountering stray dogs up there was so unlikely that I went a couple of nights without mentioning it to anybody. Then finally my friend Sid Smith said something, and everybody chimed in, "Yeah, we've been hearing that howling too."

We formed a search party and went looking on the other side of the river. The first day we found nothing, but that night we heard even more dog sounds. So in the morning we went back again—and found an old blue tick hound about half starved to death but wearing an expensive-looking collar. We gave him some cold fresh fish we were carrying for a snack, and he was as friendly and tame as if he was our own pet.

After he'd eaten, he actually seemed to want to lead us someplace. So we followed him for about three or four miles through the woods until we saw signs of what had been a camp. And there, in the middle of it all, was a dead horse, his carcass about half rotted away. A real mystery—until, just then, that dog trotted over to me and for the first time I noticed something on his collar: the name Stewart Hamlin. Not only was it an eerie coincidence because Hamlin is the name of the town where I grew up, but I knew who Stewart Hamlin *was*. He was a cowboy singer and Christian radio preacher who had his own show in California.

I called Hamlin as soon as we got back, and he explained that he'd been hunting mountain lion and had had to shoot the horse himself after the animal broke its leg while trying to make it over some rocks. I never did give the man back his dog, though. I guess that hound had a companion back in there someplace, because even though we got him to our camp that night, we continued to hear howling. And when it came time to head out, that dog only went part of the way with us. After a few hours of tagging along nice as could be, he suddenly turned and, for no apparent reason, trotted back to an environment where he didn't belong, and almost certainly wouldn't survive. The whole experience was downright eerie. . . .

. . . And certainly nothing like the time a couple of years later when we saw ice cream coming down out of the sky.

That year Andy and I had been flown into Tunnel Meadows, deep in the Sequoia National Forest, by our friend

Bob White, a pilot who ran a flying service out of Lone Pine, California. We were at the end of a long day's hike, when a thunderstorm came up. Lightning hit a clump of trees across the Kern River from where we were, setting off a spectacular fire—and we decided to spend the night right where we were. The next day we got up early and began the arduous climb up out of the Kern canyon. There are many switchbacks along the trail, and with fifty-pound packs on our backs, the going was slow and uneventful—until around noon, when we heard a Cessna come up the canyon.

"Could be Bob White's plane," I said to Andy. Then I got out my signal mirror and began to flash him from the ground so that he'd know where we were. Well, the guy wobbled his wings a bit, to acknowledge our signal, and then took off. Andy and I just looked at each other and shrugged.

"I just hope," Andy said, "that you didn't trigger some goddamn emergency search."

But as it turned out, all the pilot was doing was getting in better position to make a nice run through the canyon. And when he did a few minutes later, he passed us real low and, much to our amazement, some packages—cardboard boxes wrapped in burlap—came flying out of his side window. Andy and I immediately split up and found them with no trouble, but as soon as we did this cowboy appeared from out of nowhere, on foot, and said, "Did you see anything?"

"I sure did," I told him. "I've got it right here. It's ice cream and it's dripping like hell. We've got no spoons, but you're welcome to help us eat it."

Well, he said sure, and invited us down to this big cattle camp where he was working. On the way over there, though, Andy spotted this envelope stuck to one of the packages, and just assuming it was for us, he opened it and read it. "Dear Shorty," it said. "We'll be coming back again next Wednesday with more supplies."

"Hey, by any chance do they call you Shorty?" I said to the cowboy. "And were you by any chance expecting an airdrop today?"

"Yeah," he said, "that's what they call me. And as a matter of fact, I was waiting for some kind of delivery. How did you guys know?"

So we showed him the note. Andy felt embarrassed by the misunderstanding, but I thought it was funny as hell. Ol' Shorty didn't seem to mind, either, because he took us back to the camp and was really hospitable. In fact, when we finally got around to formal introductions, I found out that he had been the physical education instructor at Taft Air Base, where I went through basic flying school.

There's a P.S. to this story. Later, back at our own camp, we were set to hit the trail again when that same plane came droning over our heads once more. And sure enough some more packages came flying out. We picked them up—and found out they were steaks. So we carried them back to Shorty's camp.

"Looks like you boys is gonna have to stay for dinner," he said.

It was an offer we couldn't refuse.

I've got a confession to make: the idea of an illegal airdrop was nothing new to Andy and me. We certainly don't do it anymore because as we've matured we've come to take the national park regulations more seriously, but over the years there have been a few times when, with the help of our Sierra-area friends, we supplemented our trout-and-more-trout diet with beef, beer, and several other things that aren't exactly indigenous to the area.

Those airdrops were great fun, but I can remember one nerve-racking incident that convinced us to abandon that particular stunt for good. It was a miserable day for any kind of air mission. The sky was gray and low; the wind swirled and gusted; and the cold rain contained an occasional hint of hail. Andy and I, up with the dim light of dawn, were really worried. "Man, it's really stinko," Andy said.

"Yeah," I agreed. "It would be better to put the whole damn thing on hold for a day or so, don't you think?"

After all, we were not exactly dealing with a matter of national security here: this was a plan to drop steak and champagne into our Sierra campsite. It had sounded so good at the time we'd planned it: well-packaged porterhouses and splits of Dom Pérignon coming down like manna from heaven. We'd perfected the idea to the point where we were even employing little parachutes. Not only did they prevent the pulverization of the prime meat sent down by our buddy, the friendly fruit farmer from Reedley, California—they also allowed him to include such niceties as stemmed wineglasses, hors d'oeuvres, and crusty French bread. Sometimes he even thought to include a copy of *Playboy* magazine, which, when tossed casually atop any handy rock, was certain to stop some passing backpacker in his tracks.

But that day the sky looked like hell, and we were genuinely worried about our flying farmer friend, who would be maneuvering a light Beechcraft Bonanza at low altitude through the mountainous terrain. Nor were the flying conditions his only problem. After about ten years of hearing rumors about Yeager's airdrops, the park rangers were getting pretty vigilant, and they kept us under

13

close scrutiny from the moment we applied for our wilderness permits. One year, when someone snuck into a ranger camp under cover of darkness and let all the horses out of the corral, some of those rangers actually accused us of creating a diversionary tactic so that we could pack out more than our legal limit of golden trout to our friends down in Lone Pine. Can you imagine us involved in such a scheme?

The point is, though, that there was a lot of pressure on our friend that day, and it showed in his performance. Just as Andy and I figured that he probably had more sense than to go up on such a rough morning, we heard what was the unmistakable drone of that Bonanza's engine. And from out of the soupy fog there came the farmer, sweeping in from the dead-wrong direction, his little plane fishtailing wildly in the crosswinds.

"Holy Christ, Andy," I said, "he looks totally disoriented. I think he's aiming for the wrong canyon."

He was. But in his frantic desire to drop what he had and get back on the ground as quickly as possible, he missed *everything* he was aiming for. Crates, with their parachutes attached, just came fluttering down hither and yon. We scoured the mountains for hours, but in the end found only one.

Let's just say it was not the one that contained about fifteen finely marbled fillets and a neat little portable grill. Nor did we ever recover our carefully constructed "wine cabinet" brimming with champagne and expensive cheeses. Probably the bears got those.

All we knew for certain was that if anyone in the High Sierras happened to want cocktail napkins, long-stemmed wineglasses, and those fancy plastic toothpicks that look like little pirate swords, they would have to deal with us.

*   *   *

At one point back in the late fifties and early sixties, Andy and I actually managed to combine our two big passions: machines and the outdoors. This was our Tote-Gote period. The Tote-Gote was a simple, shock-absorber-less vehicle that was really a forerunner of today's trail bike. At least they were simple before we first got our hands on 'em. Andy and I modified ours, and put on special stainless steel gas tanks so that we were able to cover incredibly long stretches of trail—eighty to one hundred miles sometimes—in just a few days. One of the best things about them was that we could cover a week's worth of hiking in a weekend, and furthermore, we could carry a lot more gear into the wilderness and thus live a lot more luxuriously.

Still, even with our modifications, the Tote-Gotes were rough-riding vehicles. The motor was mounted right on the frame, which meant that they vibrated so strongly that they made your hands swell up and itch something terrible. What's more, before we became proficient on them, we tended to fall off a lot, and so we'd come roaring out of the mountains with our shins all scraped up, big knots on our legs, and with our pants ripped to shreds. Hell, we'd have to keep our battered and bloody legs held real high when we'd go riding over by the Kern River because of the lively rattlesnake population down in that area.

Andy—usually so laid back, easygoing, and sensible compared to me—became a demon on those little bikes. It was a transformation much like he underwent when he stepped into the cockpit of a P-51 Mustang—or had a few belts of Scotch. I remember one year when I took off from Edwards in an F-4 and flew over the Sierras to reconnoiter our trail, which is something I always did about a week before we were set to go up. This time it looked real bad. There had been a big rockslide during the spring

15

that had taken the trail right out. I came back feeling real dejected and told Andy, "Hey, our trip's canceled. There's about one hundred yards out there where it's sheer rockslide. We'd be trying to get through on about a sixty-degree angle. It looks like we're gonna have to forget the whole trip until next year."

Bud Anderson

I don't think I've ever seen Chuck so upset about anything as he was when he reported to me about our hiking trail being wiped out—that's how much those annual camping trips meant to him. But I told him not to worry. I had these paramedics under my command at the time; they were running a survival school for Air Force pilots. "I'll talk to my people," I told Chuck. "And they'll figure out a way that we can get ourselves across."

Well, I sent about six of them up a couple of days ahead of us—and justified the whole deal to myself by saying that they'd be gaining a lot of experience in this project that would be helpful in their military work.

When we came 'round that bend in the trail on our Tote-Gotes come Saturday morning, there they were waiting for us, and with quite an elaborate setup too. They'd strung ropes between these two big trees, and they tied on those little motorbikes of ours, which weighed about 200 pounds each. Then they winched them up on pulleys

16

and drew them across to where the trail continued. Meanwhile, we walked carefully along a little footpath they'd dug out of the rockslide.

It was great. But, of course, when we came back three days later those guys and their ropes were gone. All that was left was that extremely narrow footpath.

Once Andy got on a Tote-Gote he threw caution to the wind. From that dangerous spot where the paramedics had helped us, it was about a 2,000-foot drop—or perhaps a better word would be "slide"—over tree stumps and boulders, down to the Kern River. On our way back I didn't want to take any chances, so I got off my Tote-Gote and walked, conscious that with every step I was getting a little bit closer to where the trail picked up again, and safety. It was so precarious I didn't even want to turn around—until I heard—*goddammit!*—the roar of Andy's motorbike. I couldn't believe he was actually trying to *ride* across that narrow little strip. Needless to say, he promptly lost his balance, put his outside foot down, and found there was nothing there.

OTHER VOICES

Bud Anderson

I went flying. And the next thing I knew I was holding on to a root with one hand, and trying to keep the Tote-Gote from sliding farther down the mountain with the other. If I'd let go, I could have gone all the way down into the river, with that bike coming right behind and pushing me under. It was not, in my opinion, a very funny situation. But that didn't stop Yeager from laughing like hell as he got out his trusty parachute shroud line and began hauling first the bike and then me back up to safety.

A pilot friend of ours named Dan Sabovich once tried to build a homemade version of a Tote-Gote, with results that were magnificently disastrous. The thing had a big fifteen-inch truck wheel in back and only an eight-inch wheel in front, and tiny handlebars. It really looked weird—especially when Dan got on and contorted himself into the position necessary to ride the thing: you had to see him, sitting there in this wide-brimmed plantation hat, with his ass sticking out over the piece of plywood that he'd tied on the back so he could carry some extra baggage.

The one time Dan used this strange vehicle he had it seriously overloaded. On the way in to our Sierra campsite, it struggled and sputtered until finally his damn drive belt broke, and he was stopped dead in his tracks. Our Tote-Gotes made so much noise that we didn't realize he wasn't with us anymore until we'd gone quite a little way. So we had to go back, let him take Andy's Tote-Gote back to Porterville to get another belt, and shuttle our supplies into our campsite on the Kern River flats. It wasn't easy. But eventually everything got done and we stayed for three days, caught a lot of fish, and had some fun.

Just as we started to go out, though, more problems. Dan's drive belt broke again.

"Looks like we're gonna have to make two trips *out* of here too," Andy said. But then I got the idea that if we could tie my Tote-Gote to Andy's, and Andy's to Dan's, we might be able to pull him back to civilization.

"We'll dig in and drag you out like we're a couple of locomotives," I told Dan. "All you've got to do is hang on to that thing."

Well, those Tote-Gotes fired up with an ear-splitting roar and we began to lurch and jerk our way out with Dan in tow. It was very rough going at first, but then, after about a half hour, everything seemed to smooth out. That's when I turned my head back to yell something to Andy and saw why our load felt so much lighter.

Dan was gone! And not just Dan; his weird-looking trail bike was gone too—except for the fork between the handlebars. That one little part was just bouncing along, kind of pathetically, on the end of the parachute shroud line we'd used to tie the bikes together.

I don't think I've ever seen a funnier sight. We laughed so hard we couldn't go on. And when we headed back down the trail, we laughed even harder as we found a wheel here and a plywood board there. We knew that Dan had a real hot temper and we could picture him yelling at us, and telling us to stop, goddammit, as his bike gradually came apart. And there we were plowing ahead, not being able to hear a thing.

After a few miles of backtracking, however, we could hear him quite plainly, even before we saw him. He was just standing there deep in the wilderness, and screaming at the sky. "You sons of bitches! Why didn't you stop? You dirty sons of bitches!"

*   *   *

19

When I think of the Sierras I think of all the laughs we've had up there. And when I think of laughs I automatically remember the first time we took along our Russian friend, MiG pilot Victor Belenko. This was way along into the seventies. At our suggestion, he brought nothing but a six-dollar tube tent, which resembles a huge plastic garbage bag except that it has no closed end. You create an opening—the "tube" effect—by running a rope through it and tying each end to a rock or tree. Normally, a tube tent is a good alternative to a fancy 200-dollar backpacker tent. But that year the weather up in those mountains was just piss poor. It rained night after night and old Victor would get flooded out of that tube tent of his: from inside our cozy, tight little tents we'd hear him squishing around the camp in the middle of the night, cursing.

The days weren't so dazzling either. One dreary afternoon, we were huddled under a hastily rigged tarpaulin and actually wearing woolen ski caps as a cold rain and hailstones came down all around.

"Well, Victor," I said, noticing how miserable he looked. "How do you like our American summers?"

"Sheet," he said in his heavily accented English, pulling his hat down around his ears. "And to think I leave Siberia for *this*."

Victor was not only new to the Sierras, but he had never been on any kind of backpacking trip. "In the Soviet Union," he explained one day, "this just isn't done. We have plenty of beautiful countryside, but you can't buy sleeping bags, fishing rods, or any kind of decent equipment. And forget hunting. There are no guns available to the public." He also couldn't get over the idea that a general and a colonel, namely me and Andy, were walk-

20

ing in on foot, carrying our own stuff and cleaning and cooking our own fish. "Russian military officers would never behave like this," he said. "They'd have servants, their own packers, cooks, a whole little army of their own."

Victor made up for lost time and took to fishing with a convert's zeal. He's a tight-wound spring. I mean he is in the go position *all* the time. I'll never forget the first time he was up at our favorite lake with us. He had this pole all put together, he'd bought it at Sears, and he ties into about a four-pound golden. Well, he just turned around, laid that pole over his shoulder, and headed straight up the damn mountain. Of course the pole broke in three pieces, but meantime he had a golden flopping there on the hillside and he's hopping all over yelling with delight. He couldn't have cared less about the pole. "Hey, look, fish," he was yelling. "I catch fish!" It was a pleasure to see him so happy.

I first met Victor when I was doing some consultant work with Northrop on the development of the F-20 jet fighter, and he had been brought in to provide input on modern-day Soviet fighters and their weapons systems. Of course I knew who he was from all the newspaper stories about the young Russian pilot who had taken off one day, broken out of formation, and made it all the way across the sea to Japan. It was an incredibly courageous flight that involved leaving behind his wife and young son—and landing with a virtually empty gas tank. It had also been a tremendous intelligence breakthrough for the U.S., since we'd never had a close-up look at a MiG-25 before and now suddenly we had one that we could pull apart and inspect at our leisure.

Victor and I hit it off immediately, and I invited him to come into the Sierras with us that summer we were working together at Northrop. The reason we got along so well is that he's a natural comedian who can break up a room of grim-faced aviation experts with just a word or gesture. Back then, when he was first getting adjusted to this country, he was worried, he told me, that the American people would think badly of him for what he had done—that they would think he was a traitor to his people. He was so self-conscious that first year he went with us that a couple of times when passing hikers stopped off in our camp to say hi, he'd wander off into the woods and disappear for a while. He even made a rock shelter— an old Russian trick, he said—partly to keep dry and partly, I think, to hide from anyone who might be coming along the trail.

We talked about his feelings and I told him he was dead wrong about the public reaction. "You've made a statement about the Soviet Union with your actions and your words," I told him. "You put your money where your mouth was, and put on a display of courage and flying skill that people are going to respect, not condemn. It's the Soviet politicians and military leaders that you've really ticked off." And that was true. The Russian diplomats sent up howls of protest and demanded that their former pilot and his airplane be returned to them immediately. The American ambassadors all respectfully declined this request, and the FBI has now changed Victor's identity several times in the last few years for his own protection. Victor has made a new life here.

Victor Belenko

When I first was introduced to General Chuck Yeager, I couldn't believe he was actually standing there before me. In the Soviet Union anyone even casually interested in aviation knows who he is. I first learned about him in 1967, when I was a young pilot studying supersonic aerodynamics. Our professor, a fighter pilot who had flown against Americans in the Korean War, told us that the first man to break the sound barrier was an American named Chuck Yeager. And then he added: "None of you would stand a chance in a dogfight with this man. He's got enough combat experience to nail your asses to the ground." We were impressed.

So when that same Chuck Yeager was standing in front of me and smiling and asking me if I'd like to go fishing and hunting with him and his friend Bud Anderson, I could only fumble for words. "Well, sure," I said, "sir, General."

"Hey, let's get one thing straight from the start," he said, "call me Chuck." I was amazed, because in the Soviet Union a general, especially one who was a hero, would insist on being addressed formally, even if he was out in the woods on a hike. Rank and standing on ceremony mean nothing to Yeager. You know how he hates smoking? I once asked him, "How did you cope with those obnoxious five-star generals who came into your office puffing away and dropping ashes all over your floor?"

"I didn't cope with them," he told me. "I just told them they had to put out that damn cigarette before they came in the door."

23

I could tell, just watching him around the hangar at Northrop, where we first met, that he wasn't one of those overeducated, highly technical types, but that he had a real—what do you call it?—*gut feeling* for airplanes. He could just look at a plane on the ground and tell you how it was going to behave in the air.

We didn't talk about the MiG-25 very much, because Chuck had already retired when I "emigrated" with one to the United States, and so he wasn't part of the team that went over that plane with a fine-tooth comb. But we did discuss a lot of other planes, including the MiG-15, which he *had* flown, and which we both agreed was a really primitive piece of equipment.

When he took me up in the mountains, he was always cheerful and generous with his time and knowledge about catching the golden trout. Thanks to him, I became a pretty good fisherman. Which was a good thing because, as he often pointed out, if I didn't catch my own supper, I'd have to starve—or eat raisins.

My relationship with the Sierras has evolved over the years. Once—when I was young enough to have hair and needed to let it down—I thought of those mountains as a place for raucous fun. Then things began to change in my life. Glennis no longer had four babies to take care of: they had grown into young kids and the Sierras began to play a different role for us all.

I'd still get up there to the top when I was with Andy and some others, but shorter trips became possible with

Glennis and the kids. I was a father, and fishing and hunting was something I did with my family, a set of skills that I passed on proudly to my kids.

Glennis Yeager

Our daughter Susie is real good at fishing, and was even as a young kid. I remember one time when she was about ten or twelve, she joined in a contest at the Rod and Gun Club—all boys—and she won! She's really a good shot too. The boys, of course, are good at both hunting and fishing. Chuck used to take them with him all the time, but the girls usually didn't go all the way up in the High Sierras. We'd go on long trips though. Susie and I went with him one time, and I remember we'd brought the little poodle, Pookie, with us. We went up to Rocky Basin Lake, hiking mostly, but leading horses. I managed to break the big toe of my right foot the first night in there, stepping out of a sleeping bag onto a rock. It was bitter cold and the damn toe broke, just as if it were frozen. It was a real *ouch*! The whole foot and ankle swelled up badly. But Chuck found an old piece of tire and he made me a sandal out of it. At the time, it seemed better to rest the foot and let the swelling subside so we decided to stay. Still, I couldn't walk, so I never got to leave camp. They all took off and went up to the higher lakes and everything every day, and other places. I had to stay put.

To get out of there I had to ride a horse, holding Pookie in front of me. He wouldn't ride with anybody but me. Part of the way was straight downhill, a steep grade even for a horse, and I'm up there hanging on to Pookie with one arm, using the other hand to try to get a balance with the one foot I could put into a stirrup, and praying the horse wouldn't miss his step. . . . It was funny.

The years when Glennis and our two sons and two daughters came along were fun for me, but in a different, quieter way. We knew we were teaching our kids, especially the boys, something that our parents had taught us. And that was pretty satisfying. We'd throw packs on their backs even when they were ten and twelve, and take them out for miles to Quaking Aspen. After a while they learned that they couldn't quit on a trip like that; they had to keep walking, and then once they got deep in the wilderness, they had no choice but to make the long trek out. We'd be gone for a week or two with no TV, no candy, and we'd all really have to rough it. We had some grousing and pouting from time to time, but never any real problems. My kids all grew up with fishing rods in their hands, and as soon as they were old enough I taught them how to handle guns safely, just as my brothers and sister and I had been. My girls, Susie and Sharon, were just as good at the traditional outdoor skills as the boys.

I used to take them all hunting coyotes on the big ranches where it's allowed. I'd put Susie, who was always an especially good shot, up on a ridge and let the boys and Sharon drive the coyotes out of the brush. Susie was only about nine then, but she'd calmly sight those coyotes through her rifle scope and pick them off—*pow, pow*—one by one. Her natural skill with a gun didn't surprise me in the slightest; look at the role model she had. Glennis is a crack shot who as recently as a few years ago proved she could still handle a heavy rifle well enough to bag an elk at a couple of hundred yards.

For people raised the way Glennis and I were, it is possible—and even more than that, it's *natural*—to both love animals and hunt them too. For example, I can't count how many ducks I've shot and brought home to a woman who puts food out nearly every day for the mallards and wood ducks who live on our pond back home. (And who's death on any domesticated well-fed feline greedy enough to come hunting "our" ducks.) We don't see any conflict in that because we understand how nature works and how nature provides—providing you don't ask the environment to yield up more than it is able. The antihunting people in this country are usually city-bred types who don't know that nature itself kills more animals than any hunters ever will. It does this by natural life cycles, which can result in overpopulation of certain herds. That leads to starvation of many animals—drawn-out deaths that are minimized when state fish and game departments issue permits that allow hunters to come in and harvest the surplus deer, elk, and other game.

The key is to operate out of respect for the animals and the environment that supports them. When Glennis and I were stationed in Germany, from 1954 to 1957, and again from '68 to '70, we went on many hunting parties with Dr. Melsheimer (our guide) and his son Karl Armin—and while I never saw anything more formal outside of a White House dinner party, I'd also have to add that their way of harvesting animals was beautiful to behold. We all

27

wore dark green outfits on the hunt, and each time an animal was shot we conducted a little ceremony, turning the animal over on its side so that it could have its "last bite." Back at the hunting lodge, after the sun went down, the Germans sang beautiful old hunting songs; there was a special tune for each animal in the forest. Then we'd end the day with a robust meal of *rehruecken* (venison) or *enten* (duck). I never picked up much of the language, but Glennis quickly learned to converse in what's called "kitchen German," and with her help I was able to learn even more about that country's hunting habits. Like us, the Germans have game wardens who keep tabs on the various herds and tell hunters which ones and when they can thin out because of overpopulation. But they go a step further than we do with a kind of honor system that forbids the harvesting of perfectly conformed male animals, so that each breed can continue to improve and prosper. They seem to have done a pretty good job of game management, too, because I was told that the German forests are as full of game animals as they were a thousand years ago.

A lot of those rituals and rules were new to me, but their basic philosophy is the same as we had in West Virginia: "Take only what you need." I've never been a trophy hunter. I've been invited to hunt for elephants, rhinos, and other big game in Africa, but I have no desire to. When I shoot something, it's never so I can mount the horns on my wall—it's so I can put some food on my plate. What I harvest I use, skinning it myself and then turning it over to Glennis for butchering and packing away in the freezer. It's like the old days back in Hamlin when supper could as easily have been a beefsteak as a bear steak. Nothing gets wasted.

*   *   *

You can't hunt in the national parks where we made most of our Sierra trips, but you can fish—and that was how, as a family, we had most of our fun. After we all pitched in to catch the day's trout, we'd all help cook them in our patented Yeager way. Our favorite recipe, like the trip itself, has changed and evolved over the years. But in those early days we'd carry a big slab of bacon with us, and after we caught the fish we'd wrap it in aluminum foil with a slice of bacon and then lay it right on the coals. We didn't carry skillets back then because they were too hard to clean. (If you didn't get the pan completely scoured, it could become a breeding ground for bacteria that could make you sick—a serious problem out there in the wilderness, where it might take as much as three days to reach the nearest doctor or drugstore.) So until those easily cleanable lightweight Teflon skillets came along, we cooked on the coals and carried only an aluminum pot that we could use to boil water and maybe make soup in.

Sometimes the boys did find the diet a little monotonous, and I'll never forget the trip when they all started twitching their noses at the same time, as we got about two miles from an old shed which a pack-horse supplier named Scott Jameson used to house his animals. No one was around at the time but the boys kept sniffing and sniffing until they zeroed in on a particular tree where this delicious smell was coming from. I guess they inherited the Yeager curiosity. In any case, Mike threw a rope up into the branches and Don shimmied up—and came down with a cooked ham that someone must have hidden from the bears and then forgotten. That ham was still in great shape, though, and so they brought it down and we all gorged ourselves on that thing for two days.

2
THE WAY IT IS NOW

As the kids got older and started having families of their own, my summer trip into the Sierras became something else again. Not that it's ceased entirely to be a family affair: my sons, Don and Mike, still come along from time to time, and Andy's son Jimmy, a fighter pilot in the Air Force, will join us occasionally too. But these days those two weeks in early July are more like an annual ritual played out by two old fighter pilots.

It's still fun, only our definition of fun has changed. Andy and I use that time to prove to ourselves that we can still make the long, tough haul to our favorite mountain lakes, climbing to altitudes of nearly 14,000 feet with fifty-pound packs on our backs. Though it may sound immodest, we consider ourselves virtuoso outdoorsmen, and once a year it's satisfying to put all the skills we've acquired over the years into play and partake of what we consider to be the ultimate "back-to-nature" experience.

I want to tell you about a trip we made recently so you can get an idea of what it's like. On this one, Andy and I were supposed to have some newcomers, but they were dropping by the wayside one by one.

That was predictable—and understandable. Two weeks in the fresh air of the Sierras *sounds* good to a lot of people, but when they came right down to it, many guys had practical considerations: wives and kids who had a claim on Dad's limited amount of vacation time; or bodies that weren't up to some of the pretrip exercise routines that we recommend.

I was right about the necessity of being in shape, though. You can't just go from a sedentary life-style into a trip like we make each summer. Usually, Andy and my brother, Hal, start taking long, challenging walks months before each Sierra trek to build up their cardiovascular systems as well as their mental toughness. Meanwhile, I stay fit by jogging for a half hour each day, whether it's down Fifth Avenue in New York City or on a trail near my home. I also make sure to eat right the whole year round. It's a way of life with me by now. And yet even with the various preparations that we make, and regimens we keep, we are invariably in better shape on the way *out* of the mountains. By then, after two weeks in the high altitude, our lungs are operating at peak efficiency, and we all weight ten to fifteen pounds less than on the way in.

I try to discourage smokers from even attempting to come along; in any case, under the Yeager-Anderson rule book, they are strictly prohibited from bringing cigarettes into the Sierras. Nicotine has been a real turnoff for me ever since, at a particularly tender age, I tried to chew a twist of tobacco and was sick for a week. Andy, after having a similar experience as a kid, has never smoked either, and I don't think we could have been as close friends as we are if he or I had always had to have that weed in our hands. The smell of the stuff is bad enough, but the idea of being as dependent on something as some smokers are is what goes totally against my grain. One year a friend of ours, a California highway patrolman who lives near me in Grass Valley, didn't know how serious I was about my no smoking rule.

"You're gonna have to get rid of those before we go up in the mountains," I said, nodding to the carton of cigarettes between us on the seat of my pickup truck as we drove down to Lone Pine.

He just said something in response like "Oh, sure," but when we were ready to hit the trail, they were still there. So while he watched with a dropped jaw I shoved those damn things into the nearest trash bin, then said, "Okay, let's move it on out."

But back to our own current trip. Even though everyone else was dropping out, Hal was joining us, as he had been for the last several years. I'm glad he's become one of the regulars. Hal is a big, strapping guy who's built more like my late brother, Roy, than I am. He's got all the hunting and climbing skills you'd expect from a kid who was raised around Hamlin, in addition to being one of the flat-out best fishermen I've ever seen. He's ten years younger than I am, which means we didn't spend all that much time together when we were growing up. So, up in the Sierras, we're doing some of the things that we didn't get a chance to do back then, and having a helluva good time doing them. Hal's got the kind of outgoing personality that has served him well in his white-collar job with Union Carbide in Houston. He can construct lies with the best of 'em when we gather around our so-called bullshit fire each night. And besides that, he serves a valuable function as mediator and arbitrator, settling disputes between me and Andy over how many fish one or the other of us caught—or how far we walked on some long-ago Sierra mountain day.

It's practically an outdoors tradition to sit around swapping tales after the dishes are done, but if you don't keep yourself in line, you can lose the distinction between fiction and reality. And that can be dangerous. I can remember a time when Andy and I were working our way along the Kern River, to Horsetail Bridge. There were no trails. We kept going all morning and afternoon, and as it grew dark we had to hack our way through dense underbrush. It was getting to be one helluva long, hard haul.

"Dammit," Andy said as we trudged along wearily, "are you *sure* we can make it all the way to the bridge in a single day?"

I had to stop right there and laugh. "Well," I told Andy, wiping away the sweat that was just pouring right off me, "all I know for real sure is that I told so many people how we did it once before with no problem that I started to believe the damn story myself."

In a way, I was a little disappointed that there'd be no fresh faces on this trip. We've taken some newcomers with us in recent years and it's fun to share the experience of the High Sierras with someone who's never seen anything like it before, to catch the wonder in their eyes as they watch the sun come up over the cliffs at some mountain lake or see the first spectacular views as we make our way toward a high pass. When most people think of the ultimate vacation, they picture themselves reclining in so-called luxury beside some hotel swimming pool or being cooped up in some dimly lit casino in Las Vegas. Andy and I know there's something better.

Needless to say, anyone who's expecting a cushy, relaxing two weeks in the mountain greenery when they come along with us is in for the shock of their lives. We never invite anyone who doesn't seem up to it, and the first couple of days in the wilderness we'll watch a newcomer very closely, keeping an especially close eye on their feet. Just asking a guy how he's doing isn't sufficient to find out: almost no one wants to be the first to say, "Hey, I've had enough." So you don't listen to what's being said. You watch the way a guy's hiking boot is coming down on those rocky trails. That way you can tell whether he's really doing okay or getting real rubbery-legged and ready to take a tumble, which up there can mean a slide practically into the next county.

Even the strong don't always survive those tough first days when we walk ten hours at a stretch and the air gets thinner and thinner. A couple of years ago Hal's son, Ron, a healthy young guy who plays a lot of racquetball to keep fit, came along with us, but about the second day in from Lone Pine he began wondering if he could keep up with us old codgers. "I've got to stop," he gasped at one point, and we said, "Okay." But by the time we'd slipped out of our backpacks and started to say, "We can rest here awhile," Ron was on the ground, dead asleep. Other guys we've brought along have started off all gung-ho, and then gotten quieter and paler and more sickly-looking as we pushed upward and onward along the switchback-laden trails—until they finally have to stop and puke in the middle of all that spectacular scenery.

"What are we gonna do in another ten years, when we're both in our mid-seventies?" Andy asked me not long ago while we were both sitting on a granite boulder 13,000 feet up in the Sierras.

"Reckon we'll go back and try pack mules again," I said.

A few years ago we decided that mules made things too easy. But now they loom as a means we might use to keep coming deep into the mountains until we drop. That is, if the environmentalists will let us.

In recent years we've started making our entire trip within the Sequoia National Forest, and the trail crews do a fine job of clearing a way for us hikers. Still, there are many tough and even treacherous spots along the way, especially when we encounter a recent rockslide or a steep stretch where the ice and snow linger. Often, we find ourselves inching along a narrow ledge where a slip would mean sliding down a couple of thousand feet over tree stumps, rocks, and similar body-battering terrain. Rock-climbing tools would make things easier, but we prefer to do things the natural way, using only our well-worn hiking boots and our bare hands to get where we're going. It's not that we're gluttons for punishment. But the idea on these trips is to play the cards that the environment deals you and not rely so much on tools or technology. Or, as it says in the handbook Andy and I give out to those who express an interest in coming along, "The basic concept is austerity."

We don't take anything with us that we don't absolutely need or won't use. There have been many years, in fact, when we simply unrolled our sleeping bags under the star-studded Sierra sky each night, and never bothered with any tents. If it happened to snow during the night, as it does sometimes even in July in the higher elevations, we'd just shake the accumulation off our sleeping bags in the morning and keep going.

That handbook of ours has a way of weeding out the fainthearted. It's a no-frills fifteen-page homemade affair that Andy and I first put together in the mid-sixties and have revised several times since, the last time being in January 1987. We just print it up, and send it off each spring to any first-timers who might be thinking about coming along. There's a map on the cover, drawn by a neighbor of Hal's, of the area around Mt. Whitney where we usually camp our first night. From there we move from lake to lake, according to the state of terrain and temperature of water, but we usually climb steadily. Doing it this way, with an infinite number of variations, the lakes we might fish include, among others, Chicken Spring, Sky Blue, Rocky Basin, and we usually finish up at our favorite lake, depending on our mood and the weather. But we sometimes end our trip with an eighteen- to twenty-mile hike that takes us near the top of Mt. Whitney and back down into the little town of Lone Pine, where we almost always start.

Here's what the book looks like, and a sampling of the way it reads:

INTRODUCTION

THERE ARE probably AS MANY WAYS TO GO backpacking AS THERE ARE REASONS FOR GOING ON A backpacking trip. THIS CHECKLIST PRESENTS SOME thoughts ABOUT ONE WAY TO GO. It has been developed OVER MANY YEARS OF HIKING IN the Southern CALIFORNIA SIERRA NEVEDA mountains. THE UNDERLYING PURPOSE OF THE TRIPS is GENERALLY JUST TO GET AWAY FROM it All, MEET A CHALLENGE, KEEP IN GOOD physical CONDITION, SEE SOME BEAUTIFUL COUNTRY AND TO FISH FOR TROUT IN CLEAR FRESH WATER UNDER LESS CROWDED conditions.

THE basic CONCEPT IS AUSTERITY — — — dont take things you dont need OR will NOT USE. KEEP PACK WEIGHT TO A MINIMUM. THE CHECKLIST IS based ON A SEVEN TO FOURTEEN day TRIP IN THE VICINITY OF MT. WHITNEY DURING late JUNE THROUGH MID July.

Although perhaps NOT COMPLETE OR ADEQUATE FOR EVERYONE THIS CHECKLIST SERVES AS A basic GUIDE FOR ALL TYPES OF BACKPACKERS.

BASIC ITEMS

TARP - LT. WT. GROUND COVER,
ALSO EMERGENCY SHELTER

TENT - LT WT. TWO MAN backpacker
type with rain shield.
Plastic tube tent is a good
ALTERNATIVE, LT. WT., INEXPENSIVE
but good for one trip and it
tends to collect moisture inside

FOAM SLEEPING PAD - full length
2½" EGG CRATE TYPE DESIGN,
LT. WT - good insulation and
can be packed in small roll.

BACKPACK FRAME & CARRY BAG -
Quality LT. WT Aluminum type,
padded shoulder straps and
hip belt recommended.

MAPS - USGS Topo type maps - cut
& preassemble - fold & carry
in plastic baggie

SLEEPING BAG - Quality Lt wt.
fiber fill type (10-15°F wt)
INEXPENSIVE, EASIER TO dry out
& clean, also insulates when
WET

• TIPS:

COOKING TROUT - COVER WITH CORN
MEAL, PLACE IN TEFLON SKILLET, HEAVY SIDE TO
CENTER, COVER WITH FOIL & COOK APPX 10 MINS
PER SIDE. USE liquid MARGARINE TO add flavor
SERVE HOT OR WRAP IN FOIL FOR cold TRAIL LUNCH

PLASTIC GARBAGE BAGS :- MANY VALUABLE
USES. TIE UP FOOd & STORE FOOd hANGING FROM
A TREE AWAY FROM VARMINTS, CARRY SNOW,
POORMANS RAIN PANCHO, backPACK RAIN COVER,
USE TO WRAP FISH & TO CARRY TRASH OUT.

PACKING FISH - CLEAN FISH & PLACE
IN SNOW OR LEAVE OUT ALL NIGHT ON STRING
TO GET AS cold AS possible. WRAP IN plastic
GARBAGE bAG. PLACE PACKAGE IN THE middle
OF SLEEPING bAG ROLL. INSULATION will
KEEP FISH cold FOR mANY HOURS.

FOOT CARE - WEAR A KNOWN pAIR
OF BROKEN IN boots, CHANGE SOCKS EACH
dAY. USE tincture OF benzoin ON known
TENDER SPOTS TO TOUGHEN SkIN IN AdVANCE
OF TRIP. PUT MOLE SKIN ON CRITICAL SPOTS.
FOAM TOE CAPS ARE AvAilAble. USE liquid
bANdAdGE ON SORE SPOTS.

If you read between the lines of the booklet, you can see that trip of ours can be a real butt buster. A lot of the friends Andy and I had around Edwards, both in and out of the military, claimed to love fishing—but they thought of it as dozing in the sun with a rod in their hands. They'd talk big about coming up in the Sierras with us, until they saw our booklet or heard us go on about the trip a little more. Then they'd begin to have doubts.

"You really hike eighteen miles in one day with full packs?" they'd ask. "Hell, yes," I'd tell them. "Andy and I sometimes cover seventy-five to a hundred miles during a trip and don't think anything of it." Well, they'd look kind of thoughtful, and when the day came, they wouldn't be there waiting at the appointed spot. So Andy and I would just shrug our shoulders and go on in alone. Nothing fazes us. Not the tough walking or the sometimes violent weather. I remember one year when just the two of us were coming down through Miter Pass together and a fierce thunderstorm rolled in and kept us pinned against the side of the mountain for more than eight hours. The thunder was deafening and the lightning was striking all around us, setting these huge boulders to rolling, and when they did, they'd bounce down the rocky face of the mountain, striking off huge, fierce sparks. We couldn't move and we certainly couldn't get any fishing done. So we just huddled there in a crevice and nibbled on raisins and watched the show.

Hal Yeager

I started coming along with Chuck and Andy on their annual Sierra trip a couple of years ago, and I immediately noticed something remarkable. After all these years Chuck's combat mentality appears finally to be mellowing some. He's letting down a bit, and opening up—especially when we're up there in the mountains. Chuck and I have had very different lives. I served for two years in the Air Force, and I'm now a systems engineer with Union Carbide in Houston. I tell people I'm "the other Yeager." But the different paths we've chosen, while they may have kept us physically separated for many years, seem to make less and less difference as time goes on. Scampering over the granite boulders in the Sierras with Chuck, and fly-casting in those mountain lakes—well, it's not very different than playing cowboys and Indians on Whitaker Rocks and hauling catfish out of the Mud River back home. We're getting to be brothers again.

When July finally rolled around that year, Andy, Hal, and I hooked up, just like we always do, at the Reno airport. That may not sound like the most logical spot for us to rendezvous, what with Lone Pine, California, a six-hour drive to the southwest, but we've found it convenient for several reasons. In the first place, Reno's much smaller and calmer than LAX in Los Angeles. Secondly,

Andy and I can get there in our pickup trucks in about one and a half hours from our homes—and Hal can fly in pretty easily from Houston. Finally, Reno's a good place for me to visit if I'm going to keep up my image as a grandfather. My daughter, Sharon, and her husband, Steve Flick, live about twenty minutes from the Reno airport, and usually on the way back home I stop and see that branch of the family and check up on our grandkids, Dan, Sarah, and Jake. Glennis, I know, will always want a full report the minute I walk in the front door.

Apart from that, however, Reno and its fancy hotels and glittering casinos hold no special attraction for me. When I was going off to the War, the only advice my father gave me was when he took me aside and said very solemnly, "Son, don't gamble." I was kind of taken aback by that because gambling was something that has never been a temptation for me, then or now. Maybe it's because I've done enough risky things, in combat and as a research pilot, to get the urge out of my system. But my disinterest in slot machines, dice, and cards could also come from the fact that I could never get excited about money. I know a lot of people who grew up as poor as I did feel exactly the opposite: they dream about hitting the lottery and having big piles of gold. But money just didn't matter to me, not so long as I had what I needed to get through the day. So why should I risk losing the little bit I do need for a lot of what I don't want? (Once in a while, though, you'll find me at Harrah's Hotel, in the automobile museum. I can walk around that place for hours, marveling at the changes in body and design just in my lifetime. At the same time, it's interesting to me that the internal combustion engine has remained fundamentally the same since I first started learning how it works.)

43

On this occasion neither Hal nor Andy nor I were even interested in stopping to play the airport slot machines when we found each other by the luggage carousels. We were all in high spirits and rarin' to go off and have a good time. We had our first laugh when we saw that Hal was wearing a blue and white baseball cap that said "Don't Ask." He had it made up special for the last day's hiking, he said—and Andy and I knew instantly what he meant. On the way out of the Sierras, when you get close to civilization and reach what is a relatively heavily traveled part of the trail, all the people you pass always seem to ask the same thing: How's the fishing? How's the weather? How long were you back in there? "Instead of answerin' 'em all," Hal said, "I'm just gonna slap on this hat."

The trip to Lone Pine went by quickly, as it always does. Sometimes—when we're in a larger group and traveling in separate trucks—Andy and I pass the time on the open highway by giving each other hand signals the way we used to in our old P-51 fighter pilot days. But this time we were all in the same truck, just the three old veterans of so many Sierra trips, and so the atmosphere was totally relaxed, with no pressure to make meaningless small talk as we rode with the windows rolled down and a country-music station playing softly on the radio. Hal's "Don't Ask" hat did get us remembering the strange collection of people we've seen at the tail end of our mountain trip, just before we reach a place called Whitney Portal, where people just wander in trying to see how far up the side of Mt. Whitney they can make it in an afternoon.

"Hell, remember that goddamn band we ran into once?" I said. "The one with all those guys carrying bongo drums, flutes, and guitars."

"Yeah, but that wasn't the strangest sight I've seen in there," Andy said. "As far as I'm concerned, nothing tops the time we saw that real old guy four or five miles from any sort of civilization, walking the trail dressed in a dark blue suit, wing-tip shoes, and a necktie."

Hal thought he could top that one. "You're forgetting the gal we saw halfway up the side of Mt. Whitney," he said, "with the spike heels and the French poodle."

We laughed and reminisced like that, and in what seemed like no time at all we were pulling into Bishop, California, the town where we traditionally stopped to pick up the odd piece of camping gear or trout lure we might still be needing, and to get our fishing licenses. Then we climbed back in the truck for the last leg of the journey into Lone Pine.

In some ways Lone Pine looks like a typical Wild-West town; you can see why a lot of old cowboy movies were made in and around there. Nestled at the edge of the Sierras, it's small and isolated and built around a once-dusty main street that is now a blacktopped highway. It has cafés and saloons and a general store or two. But now Lone Pine also has a lot of motels and souvenir shops, because so many people think of the town as an ideal jumping-off point for a trip into the High Sierras.

We're not just another bunch of vacationers to the people of Lone Pine. We started coming there about thirty-five years ago, when I was stationed at Edwards and was briefly involved in a helicopter-testing project. Helicopters are kind of tricky things to test because the performance data you get at one altitude doesn't extrapolate reliably at others. For this reason, the Air Force liked to check them out twice, once at sea level, and once at an air strip in a place called Coyote Flats, up around Bishop, which was at an altitude of 10,000 feet. I flew up there in an L20 to drop off some fuel, and then on the way back I spotted this place called Tunnel Air Strip, a few miles from Lone Pine. It was just a short runway that was used to fly in supplies and some of the more well-to-do tourists.

I was curious and had some time to kill, so I buzzed it a couple of times and then landed, and roaring out from the hangar comes this guy I would later know to be Bob White. Usually people out in those rural areas are happy to see an Air Force guy when you introduce yourself by doing a stunt or a roll or something over their property. But Bob was madder than hell.

"What are you doing out here with this goddamn transport plane?" he said. "You better get out of here and right now." I couldn't snap back at him because he was only worried about my safety. "There's been a lot of bad accidents in these mountains, you know," he told me. Well, he was absolutely right about that. It's damn difficult to fly in the Sierras because of the mountains themselves and because they play havoc with the wind currents. Crashes are not uncommon. When we're way back in the wilderness, Andy and I have occasionally looked across a valley and seen a Cessna wing lying there in a snowbank, or come upon some old wooden wing spars as we make our way along the trail. Stuff like that sends a chill down a pilot's spine.

"I'll try to be careful," I told Bob. "I'm Chuck Yeager and I've been flying back here for a few years, and so I know everything you say is correct."

Sometime later old Bob visited me at Edwards Air Force Base. I gave him a ride in a T-38 and we eventually became fast friends. He died a few years ago, but it was through Bob White that Andy and I met a host of people in town, including Bob's wife, Shirley; Dave Kruger, a local high school teacher who guides people through the Sierras in the summertime; and Bill Bauer, the former principal of Lone Pine High School, who used to organize and lead pack-horse expeditions over the rugged trails. These people are more than just nodding acquaintances. Andy and I keep in touch with our Lone Pine pals during the year and always share breakfast with them on the morning before we head up into the hills. They've always been so good to us. Ray Powell, the proprietor of the Frontier Motel, always has a room waiting for us so we can come in the night before, sleep in town, and get an early start. And Dave and Bill will do us the favor of driving us, in my pickup, to Horseshoe Meadows, and take the truck back to town. Then, twelve days later, they'll come to meet us when we come out of the woods, with our tails dragging after the final eighteen-mile push, and drive us down the blacktop highway into town.

It's important to be prepared, both mentally and physically, for our kind of vacation. On the night before we're going to begin our hiking, I climb into bed at the Frontier Motel at around eight P.M. and—even though I'm usually sharing a room with Hal and Andy (how the hell could three trail rats like us handle the luxury of three different rooms!)—I'm asleep as soon as my head hits the pillow. It doesn't make any difference *what* time zone I woke up in that morning. It's all a question of mind over matter. Thanks to the Air Force, and the way I was raised, I'm a very disciplined individual. In all my years of traveling I've never suffered from jet lag because I have developed the ability to actually will myself to sleep at a certain time, and stay sleeping until the next morning. It's just a trick I picked up during my career, but it's very valuable.

By being able to fall asleep at will, I'm on the local schedule from the moment I arrive.

Discipline—and precision—is what the Sierra trip is all about at this point in my life. Whereas once these trips represented a release, a wild weekend in the wilderness with a bunch of guys, or a family outing with the kids, now they have evolved into something more like military missions. After years of experimentation and modification, the planning has become that precise, the idea being to eliminate all things not strictly necessary to our well-being, and to keep risks to a minimum. I don't go to bed on the night before our hike begins without transferring my clothes, fishing tackle, and camping gear into my backpack. Then I make sure to check the backpack of any newcomers we might have along—and start unpacking what is invariably one overstuffed piece of equipment. Man, you should hear the howls of protest when I pull out their favorite sweater or their backup pair of designer blue jeans. It's hard to convince some guys that they can get by with just one pair of jeans for two weeks, and one shirt, but there's just no room for the extra weight. On the other hand, our rules don't eliminate the possibility of clean clothes.

"Once we get camped near a stream," I tell the new guys, "you can always take off your clothes and run a rope through the leg of your pants, or the sleeve of your shirt. Then you tie one end of the rope to a bush and drop the clothes in the water, where the current kind of agitates them and gets them pretty clean without soap."

Andy, Hal, and I have a million little tricks like that. We know how to avoid the ankle sprains, intestinal illnesses, and otherwise minor mishaps that, because of our distance from the nearest doctor at certain points during the two-week trek, could easily turn a backpacking trip into a disaster. We take great pride in not just surviving in the wilderness, but doing it with some kind of style. That's why we take a razor with us and have a camp rule about shaving every third day. We also wash our socks, bathe in the lakes with special biodegradable soap, and generally try to keep as neat an appearance as possible. It's another form of discipline and I guess it, too, harks back to Andy's and my military training. In the end, though, being neat and relatively clean makes us feel more comfortable and generally better about ourselves. I recall how we got a big kick out of it once when, on the way out, we passed a park ranger who said, "So, guys, you've been back there for the weekend." As it turned out, that was one of our marathon years: when he saw us we'd been back in the wilderness for a solid month.

Here is a page from the booklet showing exactly what provisions we bring with us, and the amounts required for a typical two-week trip:

•FOOD:

INSTANT TEA MIX, hot & cold drink
INSTANT COFFEE
CEREAL - INSTANT CUP type
SOUP   - INSTANT CUP TYPE
LEMON JUICE - RECONSTITUTED
SALT & PEPPER
SACCHARIN TABLETS, SUGAR SUB., LT wt.
VITAMINS - GEN. PURPOSE, LYSINE ¢, C
MARGARINE - Liquid type
CHOCOLATE - POWDERED drink
COFFEE MATE - MILK SUB drinks - CEREA.
BOUILLON CUBES - VARIOUS FLAVORS
Noodles - INSTANT CUP TYPE (Top Rahman
TRAIL MIX - fruit, Nuts, granola, etc.
FRUIT - dried, RAISINS & PRUNES
BEEF JERKY.
CORN MEAL.
LUNCH - first day only, SANDWICHES

BASIC FOOD IS FRESH TROUT -------

Obviously, that's not enough for three or four grown men to survive on. But since we must make the arduous climb carrying everything on our backs, it's all we can afford to carry. Besides, as it says elsewhere in our little manual, "The basic food is golden trout." Except for breakfast, when we eat the instant oatmeal with maybe a handful of raisins tossed in, we rely on that fish, breaded in a little cornmeal and cooked up our special way, to get us through the two-week trip. It's delicious and good for you. And to make up for the fact that it's not the most well-balanced diet in the world, we bring along multipurpose vitamin capsules and extra vitamin C tablets, which we make sure to take with our morning decaf.

In short, the whole damn experience is so healthy it probably could kill you. And so on the morning that we begin our ascent we make sure to load up on bacon, sausage, eggs, and all those other things we won't even have the opportunity to taste for the next two weeks or so. It's fun, but as we dawdle a bit over our second cup of coffee I always begin to get a little edgy, especially when I look up at that pay phone on the wall. I'm just dying to get out of reach of civilization and up into the Sierra foothills.

In the old days, when I was stationed at Edwards, I had to leave a map and itinerary behind so I could be reached in case of emergency. Sometimes our pilot buddies would check out our location and then swoop down in their F4s just to see how we were doing—and we'd signal "Hi" to them with the pocket-size mirrors we always carry for use in emergencies but mostly for shaving. We always got a kick out of those jet-powered visitors—even if the park rangers objected to the buzzing—and it was fun to see them. But one time a buddy of ours buzzed us and dropped

51

a roll of toilet paper, which unraveled as it came down, until it looked like a giant streamer. We knew it wasn't a gag; the toilet-paper method is in fact a sensible way of getting a message from an airplane to someone on the ground, because as the roll unwinds it's so easy to see. And sure enough, when we found the end of the streamer, there was a message in the cardboard tube. It said a pilot in my squadron had just bailed out, and I was needed back at the base immediately. A helicopter would be coming along shortly to take me back to Edwards. I remember standing there with that toilet-paper roll in my hand and saying to Andy, "Oh, damn. Duty calls."

When we stepped out into the sunbaked main drag of Lone Pine on this fine July day, something told me that we'd finally made it—there'd be no interruptions this year. And standing there in the heat that would easily reach one hundred degrees by midday, and seeing those snowcapped mountains in the distance, I knew this was about as good as life gets.

"Well," I said, squinting toward the incredible vista, "here we go again."

And so we did, marching and trudging along, moving steadily up into the thinner air. I stayed in front, with Hal tucked in behind me and Andy bringing up the rear. The going wasn't particularly bad, but it was tough enough so that we didn't do much talking. We just put our heads down and walked up and up those rocky trails. I didn't turn around for a couple of hours, and when I finally did, I got quite a surprise. There was Andy all ashen-faced, obviously suffering from the altitude and the exertion.

"Okay, break time," I said.

Do I sound kindly? In fact, I was ticked off.

"Anderson," I said, "I hope you didn't come up here in some kind of lousy shape, goddammit."

"Yeager," he told me as he slumped down on a rock and slipped out of his backpack, "go to hell."

I couldn't help breaking into a smile.

"You want a sourball?" I said, reaching into a side compartment on my pack.

"You chop-busting son of a bitch," Andy said. He was staring at the ground. Then he paused, looked up at me, and added, "Is it green?"

After about a twenty-minute rest, Andy's color came back and he seemed acclimated. He got up, slipped into his pack, and tramped along down the trail like his old self.

We reached our favorite lake on the third day and the fishing was good, but not spectacular. Hal caught the first golden using a Mepps #2 spinning lure, a fingernail-size oval of highly reflective metal that twirls and flutters as you reel it through the water. I caught the next fish, which was about the same size as Hal's, using my fly-casting rod and a dry fly from a set that was hand made by my son Mike. He's a self-taught artist who painted many of the of mallard ducks and Canada geese canvases that hang in our living room in Grass Valley. Mike has been making these cunningly real-looking artificial insects since he was about twelve years old. He does it the old-fashioned way, using fur and feathers and tying them in a way that fools even a suspicious fish such as a golden trout.

Just after Hal and I caught our first fish of the trip, Andy hauled in another bronze and red beauty using a yellow-colored lure. Now the pressure was off; we were set for supper. We continued to fish, though, because stalking the rare golden is, like most fishing, a matter of constant experimentation, and we wanted to see what was working.

Just why fish bite is a matter of continuing controversy among fishermen—whether fish hit a lure because they are hungry, or because they are mad that something else has invaded their nervously staked-out bit of territory, or just because, like Mt. Everest, it's there. All I can say for sure is that there have been years when red lures seemed to excite them more than yellow, when silvery lures seemed to work better than those with fur and feather attached— and vice versa. Sometimes dry flies do the trick, and sometimes there are more effective options. And sometimes we've had to put all our lures and flies away and bait our hooks with insect larvae we dig out of the soil at the lake shore.

Here is the page from our booklet listing what to bring in the way of fishing gear:

FISHING GEAR:

FISHING ROD - backpack break
down type - Lt Wt SPINNING
ROD

FISHING REEL - MITCHEL 300/308 type

SPOOLS - 4-6-8lb /INE, EXTRA /INE

FISHING CREEL - CARRY bAG

LEADERS - 2, 1, ¾ lb test

SNAP & SWIVELS - VARIOUS

SPINNING LURES - MEPPS type, VAR.

FLIES - MANY & VAR. TYPES & SIZES

CASTING BUBBLES

SHOT WEIGHTS - VARIOUS

PLIERS - SMALL

HOOKS - ASSORTMENT

BAIT OPTIONAL (WORMS & EGGS)

KNIFE - OPTIONAL - USE POCKET KNIFE

HOOK SHARPENER

SPARE REEL HANdle, ONE PER PARTY

REEL LUBE & REPAIR KIT - ONE PER PARTY

FISH STRINGER

Those are the tools. Whether you're going to catch any fish with them, though, depends on the way the sunlight is hitting the water; whether the wind is rippling the water surface and thus rendering the fisherman virtually invisible to the fish; the water temperature; the time of day; and a half-dozen other variables.

The golden trout is definitely not an easy fish to catch. After a season or two of trying, we learned that about the only time you can be really successful is just after the lakes break up from their winter freeze. If you don't go for them during those two weeks after the ice disappears, which is their spawning period, those fish swim on out to the deepest part of the lakes they inhabit and refuse to take any kind of lure, fly, or bait. Because you can hardly see them or feel them hitting the line, during the better part of the summer months a lot of people who fancy themselves as environmentalists simply assume the golden trout is endangered or even possibly extinct, which is sheer bull.

All I'll say is we haven't gone hungry yet. Andy and I have even noticed that the golden have gotten bigger and more plentiful in the thirty-odd years since we first came into these parts. The trick is, you've got to know where to do your fishing and—just as important—when.

And that's where being pilots was a big advantage for Andy and me. From up in the sky we could judge the state of the snow cover, and see just when the lakes were beginning to thaw. We also learned that because the lakes are at different elevations and have varying protection from the sun, they don't all break up at the same time. So we'd start our fishing at Rocky Basin Lake, then move on maybe to Funston Lake, or Sky Blue, then go from there on up to Wallace, planning our moves precisely so that

The Sierras: Chuck with golden trout; Bud in background gesturing that he's the one who caught it

Hal, Chuck, and Bud backpacking

Bud and the homemade "Tote-Gotes," used for carrying supplies into the Sierras

Golden trout for supper—and breakfast, and lunch

Bud with former Russian pilot
Victor Belenko

Mike Yeager with
backpack

Susie Yeager, aged about 13,
with golden trout

Chuck with golden trout,
caught at their favorite lake
in the Sierras

Susie and Glennis
on horseback

Chuck, Victor, and Bud on
trip when Victor first learned
how to fish

Typical golden trout
country

Chuck and Bud coming
out—the backpacks are a
lot lighter when you leave

Getting to the top—in the vicinity of Mt. Whitney

we hit each spot when it was absolutely ripe for fishing. It varies each year.

I'm sure glad that cooking the fish is a more exact science than catching them. We've experimented with a lot of methods over the years, sometimes with disastrous results. One year before we went up, Andy was bragging about this new kind of fry pan he'd discovered; it had a miraculous nonstick surface and was made in Korea. Real cheap too. Well, we toted a couple of those things way up in the mountains, put them on the grill, and, believe it or not, that goddamn miraculous nonstick surface just dripped off into the fire.

Another time I asked the guys in the sheet metal shop over at Edwards if they could make us a good backpacking grill.

"I got just the thing for you," one of them said, and he grabbed this big piece of aluminum and began hammering. When he was finished we had this handsome-looking grill, about two feet long and a foot wide, and light as a feather. Perfect for packing into the mountains.

We took that thing back up in the high country, set it up on a big rock, and lit a fire under it—and it melted.

Several years ago we finally settled on a way of cooking that suits us all just fine. The key element, besides the trout, is a good-quality heavy-duty Teflon skillet. We cover the fish with cornmeal, squirt in a little liquid margarine (which doesn't spoil as easily as butter), drop in the fish, then cover the pan with foil and cook the fish about ten minutes on each side over a medium-high campfire. Then we season it with a little lemon-flavored pepper and serve it up hot—or we let it cool down, wrap it in foil, and carry it with us for an excellent trail lunch. The golden has salmon-colored flesh and a delicate flavor that, to me, sometimes tastes like chicken and sometimes like lean pork. But one thing's for sure, I've fished all around the world and never eaten anything better.

But if our recipe for golden trout has changed some in recent years, most things about our Sierra trip haven't. Nowadays shoe stores are always featuring some new kind of high-tech hiking boots. Well, they may be good, but we stick to our old $39.95 standbys. It's the same with our tableware. Golden trout may be food fit for the gods—but we eat it off plain old tin pie plates for the simple reason that they are cheaper and just as good as the special backpacking utensils they sell in the camping supply stores. It's like that old saying: If it ain't broke, don't fix it. When something works for us, then we stick with it, even if it has gone out of fashion.

The Sierras tend to mock the whole idea of time as we know it in our day-to-day lives, and in doing so, the mountains put things into perspective. A century up there means nothing; it's less than the blink of an eye. If you could have taken a picture of these mountains in, say, the late 1880s (or even the 1380s) and matched it with a current one, you would see that—except for a rockslide here or a lightning-induced forest fire there—nothing has changed. And as long as we are sensible about protecting the environment, it will never change. The seasons will always come and go, sometimes gently, sometimes violently. The herds of deer will prosper and then hundreds starve to death in winter simply *because* they have prospered. The cycles of nature will not be denied; they remain constant and they remind us that no matter how big our problems in life seem to be, life must go on.

"God, we've had some fun up here," I said to Andy one morning toward the end of our mountain trip.

58

"You know, it's funny," Andy said, "I was just thinking how I feel so damn sorry for all the guys who never came with us."

"Yeah," I said, smiling, "ain't that the truth."

"For chrissake, will you guys stop moving!"

That was Hal. He was trying to take our picture under a particular foxtail pine tree near one of the lakes, and we weren't making it easy for him. He was trying to pose Andy and me just so, because we wanted to duplicate a snapshot taken of us in 1956 on the exact same spot.

Finally the camera clicked.

"I've got it," Hal said.

Andy and I broke out of our pose and then, without saying anything, we began moving down the trail toward our camp.

Once there, we made supper and sat around bullshitting for a while. Not for too long, though; everyone is ready for bed pretty early on these trips.

The campfire was going out and the others were stumbling off to their tents as I fumbled around in my backpack, reaching down past the multicolored sourballs and the nylon parachute line I use for stringing up tents and tarpaulins in the wilderness. Yes, there they were: the flares I had been issued by the Air Force in Vietnam. They were given to pilots so if you were forced down in the Southeast Asian jungle you could alert friendly aircraft to your position. But now, high in the mountains of California and more than fifteen years after the "use-before" date stamped on the package, those skyrockets were little more than a memento of that war in which I had flown some 120 combat missions.

I wondered if they still worked.

Shoot, they better, I thought as I shot one off. After all, it *was* the Fourth of July.

A second later there was a sharp hissing sound and the flare went up in spectacular fashion, leaving a trail of pinkish sparks. It arched over the lake and disappeared behind some huge granite boulders. For an instant the sky was lit up like a rosy dawn, the lake reflecting silver-pink.

"Goddamn you, Yeager," said a familiar voice coming from the direction of Andy's tent. "Don't you know this is a national park? You shoot any more fireworks and the ranger will be up here to throw our asses out."

I laughed softly, and I guess Andy heard me, because a big wet snowball—scooped out of one of the drifts that stay year-round in the higher elevations—suddenly whizzed by my head.

Then it was dark and serenely quiet again, as it had been for the last million years and probably will be for the next million.

I didn't follow the others into the tents. Instead, I sat up awhile. I thought some about what was happening back in Hamlin, where I'd been to see my mother four months before, in the spring. I listened to the Sierras' special silence, a quiet that never fails to put everything in my life into proportion.

And eventually, I turned in.

3

SPRINGTIME
IN HAMLIN

"In some ways," my sister
Pansy Lee was saying on the phone from Hurricane, West
Virginia, "Mom's doing just fine."

Pansy didn't have to say any more.

"Hold on a minute," I told her, "I'm getting out my
appointment calendar to see when I can get down there."

That's the way I am. If our mother, who was then living
in a nursing home in our old hometown of Hamlin, had
taken "a turn for the worse"—as Pansy had said just a
moment before—I wanted to find out exactly what that
amounted to. Two months before, right around Christmas, when I'd stopped by to see my mother with homemade jellies from California, she'd been talkative and
alert, calling me "Charles" the way almost nobody else
does anymore, and acting just as proud as punch about
the new vocational training center in Hamlin that the
county had decided to name after me. I couldn't see how
she could have slipped that far so fast. As much as I
respected and understood Pansy Lee—a strong, proud
woman in her early sixties who had a West Virginia way

61

of dealing with the truth head-on—I just wasn't going to be satisfied with a mere *description* of the situation. I had to see things for myself.

I guess I've always been that way. There's just something inside me that makes me want to check things out on the spot, hands-on, in person.

Right then, fortunately, I didn't need Glennis's schedule-juggling skills to figure out how to fit a trip back home into my schedule. I already had a commitment on the calendar that brought me back that way, and I could easily make a side trip to see Mom.

"I can be at your door at ten o'clock next Monday morning," I told Pansy as I checked out my well-thumbed appointment calendar. "We'll drive on down there together, take the grand tour of ol' Lincoln County, and go where the tourists don't go."

"Okay, Charles," said Pansy, laughing because what I was referring to was, and still is, the poorest county in the poorest state in the union. Then, kidding me right back, she added, "I'll start the leather britches cooking right now."

"You sure better," I said.

Leather britches.

Man, it had been a long time since I'd thought about those West Virginia-style green beans. In late summer we'd pick them from our garden and air-dry them in the barn. Then (or sometimes years later; they stored so well in that leathery-looking shriveled-up state) we'd boil those old beans in big iron pots for hours on end till they were ready to eat. Glennis hated the musty-earth odor that spread through the whole house as they slow-cooked on top of the stove. But to me that meant good eating and vivid memories.

Every so often, when I hear myself referred to as "General Yeager," or look around and notice that I'm the guest of honor at some fancy dinner, it strikes me that I've come a helluva long way from Hamlin. You know, back in grade school my nickname was Charlemagne, or Charles the Great, not that I was dreaming of conquering any new worlds. Big cities like Charleston and Huntington were just faraway places fraught with potential embarrassment as far as I was concerned.

When I was about thirteen, my eighth-grade class took a trip to Charleston and stopped to have lunch in a diner. I'd never been so far from home—about fifty miles, and the whole experience seemed exotic in a nerve-racking kind of way. "What kind of bread you want that sandwich on?" I remember the waitress asking me in that busy restaurant. She meant white, rye, or whole wheat, but I'd never heard of such things.

"Light," I said nervously—using our backwoods term for store-bought bread.

Now she was the one who was confused. "White?" she said.

"No, light bread," I insisted. And so it went, round and round like that, with me wishing I had stayed back home in Hamlin.

The area I hail from is real hillbilly country, a land of rolling hills that are densely wooded with pines and beeches that protect and provide for a population of squirrel, raccoon, and deer—just about enough to support the steady hunting that used to keep the wild harvest thinned down. Minor rivers (like the Mud) meander through the landscape. These dark, slow-moving waterways tend to overflow each spring, forcing people from their homes and doing much damage—but also, when they recede, leaving the bottom land along their banks rich and fertile.

The only real problem with that bottom land—as you can clearly see driving the two-lane potholed local roads—is that it just doesn't go on for very long. A farmer can't hardly get his tractor rolling when another hill juts up and hems him in. It's damn hard, if not downright impossible, to grow enough corn or tobacco on those small, irregularly shaped patches of land to support one family, never mind selling your crops commercially. And a Lincoln County man can't readily quit the land and get a job in a factory, you see, because there's virtually no industry out that way.

The sights along the back roads of West Virginia speak of a severe way of life. Even the road itself—all patched up as it is, and badly graded—tells a story of the corrupt politicians of the past, who sold off the state's natural resources of gas and coal to line their own pockets—and gave the people of West Virginia little or nothing in return.

I've visited Hamlin several times a year to see Mom. So I've kept up with the area even though I haven't lived there myself in more than forty-seven years.

To get to Hamlin I usually fly into Charleston. In the years since I've been gone, the state capital has changed dramatically. Not that long ago it was a sleepy town without much traffic and just one major bridge over the Kanawha River, which runs through the middle of the city. That bridge is kind of special to me because, not long after I'd broken the sound barrier, I flew under it in a P-80 jet—a stunt that ticked off the town fathers but gave people in those parts something to talk about for years afterward.

Today Charleston is teeming with traffic, and there are all kinds of new bridges over the river, including one that has to be repainted every couple of years because it stands too close to a chemical plant. The plant apparently emits something into the atmosphere that peels the pigment off right down to the bare iron girders.

Progress.

Such signs of twentieth-century civilization become less evident very quickly as you drive southeast from Charleston and the buildings thin out and the green hills of West Virginia begin to dominate the landscape. Every so often you might see a weathered old barn still sporting Mail Pouch tobacco signs, or a few chickens scratching and pecking around in a front yard. You might even spot an old farmer, in baggy big overalls, breaking up his field with a horse-drawn plow.

And one thing for sure hadn't changed.

"I bet this damn so-called highway's only about seven feet across," I told Pansy Lee as we headed down from Hurricane to Hamlin in my rented Chevy Celebrity. "I swear, anyone who learns how to drive on these skinny, twisty little roads, the way I did, has got to have the makings of a pretty good pilot."

She smiled. "Well, yes. But some of these bends in the road bring back memories, though, don't they, Charles?"

Pansy was right. It was a beautiful, crisp day, right at the beginning of spring, and every time we'd go over a hill and come on another of those views you get only in West Virginia, I'd start remembering about when we were kids growing up.

High up and to the right, there was the rock outcropping where an ancient spring bubbled up out of the earth. On family outings Dad used to park the car right here and us kids would scamper up there with empty jugs. We'd fill them with the coolest, clearest water you ever tasted, talking all the while about the Indians who we were just sure had gotten water there long before us. Up ahead, there was the field from which Roy and Hal, Jr., and I had stolen watermelons. And a bit farther down, a little bridge over a small stream where Dad and I used to hunt for turtles; those turtle legs make good eating, especially when there's a Depression on. . . .

My roots go deep into those hills. By looking in our old family Bible, where the birth and death records were kept, I've been able to trace the Yeagers (originally a German name that means "hunter") back to Frank, my great-grandfather.

I know when Frank Yeager lived, but where he lived exactly you could never say. He came and went from this world without ever having an address; he was just "back up in the hollers," far from any sort of civilization, a real-life hillbilly. Big Frank, as he was known, probably grew his own tobacco and corn, ate possum, squirrel, or catfish for supper most nights, and sipped moonshine whiskey.

I know for sure, from checking the old Bible records, that he had twenty-five children by at least two different wives.

One of his sons was Marion Yeager. That was my grandfather. Grandpa Yeager moved the family a step closer to the twentieth century to an area known as the Panther Branch of the Mud River. He had a frame like hay wire, tough and skinny, and he sported only one eye. With my dad away in the natural-gas drilling fields six out of seven days most weeks, I'd go see Grandpa often and he became an important figure in my life: my first real hero.

It was Grandpa Yeager who taught me so much about how the natural world works, how to hunt and fish and find shelter, that I could have survived, in style, alone in the woods, from the age of about eight onward.

You just *had* to learn to live off the land if you lived around Hamlin because money was in such ridiculously short supply. It's hard for a modern city-bred person to conceive of this, but someone like Grandpa Yeager might make only a few hundred dollars a year in cash. To get by, he had to trade tobacco for some flour, corn for salt or other basics he couldn't grow for himself, and harvest the rest from nature.

From Grandpa Yeager I learned that the forest is made up of interlocking systems. There are certain trees, like beeches, he told me, that furnish food for squirrels—and certain areas where the briars and brush are a natural home for rabbits. He'd tell me that we needed to keep those areas intact, because the animals in them gave us everything from food to warm clothing. A man like Grandpa Yeager knew that if you didn't use the forest wisely, you were only hurting yourself.

He didn't know a lick about "environmentalism"; for him good forest management was just common sense. I used to love watching Grandpa cut shakes, or house shingles, out of cedar and oak. He went about it very economically, cutting down only the very straight trees for his shakes because that meant the grain of the wood would be straight and not have any knotholes in it. He didn't let the trees he'd cut dry out much before he got to splitting the shakes, because then they got tougher to cut. And finally he stacked and dried his shakes so they wouldn't warp. Just seeing all those extras stored alongside of his house gave me a sense of security.

It's like the line I say in those TV commercials for AC Delco auto parts: "Don't wait for trouble to happen." I didn't get that from some Madison Avenue ad writer; it came from Grandpa Yeager, who always had plenty of shakes ready so we'd be warm and dry even if some kind of trouble came.

Chestnut trees are just about gone from the American

landscape now, wiped out by the great blight in the 1930s that killed most of them in just a few years. But when I was a kid, Grandpa Yeager had plenty of them on his property and I'd help him harvest the nuts each fall, going up, barefoot and shirtless. I'd pick whatever I could. Then I'd shake the limbs to get the ones I couldn't reach.

This was one of the many ways we brought natural foods to our table. But harvesting those nuts was something else too: a lesson about life. I learned something important about myself when I first started going up in those chestnut trees at about the age of five.

What made chestnut harvesting a challenge was that the outside shell of a chestnut is covered with big, ornery-looking burrs and when you shake 'em down, they strike your bare skin and stick right into you. Hurt? Hell, those chestnuts made me want to really scream out loud. I had to weigh the pros and cons of the deal. If I shake this tree, I'd say to myself, I'm gonna be hurting bad. But on the other hand, those chestnuts taste real good. What to do?

I remember sitting up there in the branches for a few moments before I finally said to hell with the pain—and shook those chestnuts down on myself. Sure enough, it hurt so much that I cried. But then the worst was over. I stopped crying and went on down and picked up my chestnuts.

I learned something about myself right then and there that has been proven over and over again in combat and research flying: I'm the type of person who is inclined to take a risk and go for it. When those prickly chestnuts were raining down on me it wasn't pleasant. But I realized even then that fretting over how much it hurt was just a waste of time. Worrying didn't make me feel any better. And it sure didn't make any chestnuts hop off that tree.

*   *   *

The Yeagers were never a family to wallow in self-pity. Pansy's cheerfulness—when I'd first spoken to her about Mom's condition, and now that I was down there with her—was another reminder of home. A widow since 1977, when her husband died of cancer, Pansy was being true to her Yeager roots—that is, she was not optimistic, not pessimistic, just realistic.

Let me explain what I mean by that. From living so close to the natural world, and depending on it to a great degree in our youth for food, shelter, and clothing, we Yeagers are totally at peace with the idea that everything changes; life has its seasons and its cycles. People move away from your hometown, and new folks come in. Your kids grow up and leave the nest. And yes, your loved ones get old and sick, and eventually die. Mom did seem to be slipping fast, it was true. But the plain fact of the matter was, Susie Mae Yeager was eighty-nine years old. She had lived her life the way she wanted to, raised four children to adulthood and survived the tragic death of a fifth. There was no reason to feel sorry about my mother's life—or that our natural concern for her was bringing at least part of the family together for this spur-of-the-moment visit.

We might as well enjoy the visit—and so we did. Pansy Lee lives in a nice ranch-style home that she and her husband, Billy Cummings, an executive with the local gas company, built in the early '70s, about five years before he died. It sits, surrounded by a manicured lawn, at one end of Hurricane, a town that despite its folksy name, is actually a bedroom community for a lot of people who hold down white-collar jobs in Charleston.

Just by walking around her place you can tell that Pansy's a grandmother. There are pictures of her daughter Tisha's little boy all over the house. Pansy is a "keeping" kind of person. On a little table that stands in her parlor there's the very same china tea set she herself used to play with as a child.

"You sure do save things, don't you?" I said.

"C'mon down to the basement," she said, waving me past the first floor guest room. "I want you to see something."

At first I couldn't imagine what she meant. I'd already been in Pansy's rec room, which she'd finished with solid oak paneling that had once been part of our uncle Lindsay's barn. (Lindsay didn't get it new either; we Yeagers hate to waste anything, especially if it's made of good wood.) I knew from her letters that she'd hung a colorful little quilt I'd given her—a map of West Virginia with the location of Hamlin clearly marked. Now I saw something big, dark, and wooden hanging above a sofa. At first it looked like an oar. But then I saw that it was the old wooden stirring stick Dad had hand-carved for Mom, probably back in the depths of the Depression.

"That's what Mom used to make apple butter with," Pansy said proudly.

"Well, it sure is," I said, reaching over to run my fingers down its length. Apple butter. I could have lived on that stuff for years. It was pinkish and sweet, and like almost everything else in Hamlin, a lot of hard work went into making it.

You could still see the dark spots on the handle where Mom gripped it as she mashed those apples in the kettle. After they'd cooked a spell, she'd pour in the sugar and simmer that apple mash until it turned reddish and had the consistency of jam. Then we'd slather it on a hunk of homemade bread. Sometimes it was a treat, and sometimes, when times were tough, it was supper and we'd eat as we worked.

We were never fancy or formal about meals back home. We'd usually be doing our chores, sloppin' hogs and weeding the garden, when Mom or Grandma Yeager rang the dinner bell. Then we'd sit down and eat all together—but quickly—and go right back to milking cows and putting the chickens into their coops for the night. On Sunday, the one day of the week Dad was home from the gas-drilling fields, we might have company over and there would be some talking. But even then we didn't linger around the dinner table. All our socializing was done out on the porch, while Mom and Grandma washed the dishes. "Go on, git," Mom would say if she caught you dawdling at the table.

And that never changed. Even after I became well known, there was no bowing and scraping or serving me on silver platters when I went home. Mom treated me like I was just the same old Charles. It wasn't that she didn't think I was special, because she always had tremendous faith in me. I'll never forget a few years ago, when there was a movement afoot to have me run for the U.S. Senate from West Virginia. Someone asked her what she thought about it and she said, "Whatever Charles sets his mind to, he can do." I quickly came to the conclusion that a Senate seat would put a crimp in my life-style, and so I never pursued the matter. Still, the way she spoke those words, she obviously had no doubt that I could go as far as I wanted in politics. But treat me like King Tut at the dinner table? In the Yeager household it just isn't done.

As I watched Pansy pack up what would be that day's lunch, I realized that there might have to be a few extra miles of jogging in my immediate future. Pansy had put together the best part of an all-out country meal to take down to the home where Mom was staying: in addition to leather britches, there were boiled spareribs, corn, two kinds of bread, and butterscotch pie.

"Mom may have lost something of her concentration," Pansy said, "but she's still got an appetite."

She was dolloping whipped cream on those pies as she spoke. All I could do was smile and say, "Apparently so."

Pansy had all her covered dishes and pans packed in boxes in just a few minutes, and then it was time to go. There was one more thing I wanted to see, though, and while Pansy went to get her jacket I wandered down the hall and into her guest room. There on the bed was one of Mom's hand-sewn quilts. They were made from scraps of flour sacks and sugar sacks. Those sacks used to come all printed up with flowers, or stripes, or whatever, and everybody reused them to make blouses, aprons, even dresses. Then the leftover bits were used for quilting. I've always thought there's nothing more soothing to the eye than sunlight streaming through a window and striking one of those beautiful spreads. The colors seemed as subtle as ever, even after fifty years. And the delicate circular stitching shows that Mom wasn't just a workhorse who did all the heavy work while her husband was away. She was also capable of producing what some people would consider honest-to-goodness folk art.

Quilting was normally a social function, with a bunch of ladies getting together to sew on the same item, and talk. But Mom was so particular about her quilts that she didn't want anyone else helping her with the stitching, even if it was breaking the unwritten rules.

"Mom mentions these quilts every once in a while," Pansy called from the kitchen. "She talks as if she's coming home to them someday."

I just shook my head. "They're sure pretty," I said,

running my fingers over the old fabric. "Remind me, when we're down there with her, to tell Mom how we were admiring them."

From Hurricane it was a half-hour drive through the still-beautiful countryside on those old narrow, curvy roads that connect Hamlin with the outside world. West Virginia resembles northern California in some ways, but on a much smaller scale. While I live in the pine-covered foothills of the Sierras, West Virginia sits on the Appalachian chain, where the rolling hills have a gentle, more weathered look than California.

High on the tallest hill in Hamlin sat Mom's nursing home. Or so I call it. In fact, it is a clean and handsomely furnished private residence where she has stayed these last few years—one of only two older ladies who are taken care of by Sylvia, a local woman in her mid-forties. Sylvia is a great country cook (her specialty is candied sweet potatoes) as well as a cheerful and tireless caretaker. She helps her two lady guests get dressed, feeds them if they can't manage themselves, and washes and sets their hair at least twice a week. Yes, Mom sometimes talked about someday going back to her own place: the modest, light green house that Dad built for them after the War. It's located a short distance from where she is now, and directly across the street from the rambling white house where we all were raised. But her days of being able to live alone are over. And besides, she couldn't be more comfortable than she is with Sylvia.

I pulled my rented Chevy into the driveway.

Sylvia was at the door to greet us. Then she stepped aside and ushered me into the living room, where Mom sat in her wheelchair.

*   *   *

Probably most men carry around mental pictures of their mothers, and that picture is usually of a woman in her prime. The Susie Mae Yeager of my boyhood days obviously came from hardy, rural stock. She stood about five feet seven, had broad shoulders and strong arms suitable for hauling wood and heaving around the hundred-pound feed sacks for the hogs, cows, and chickens that we raised. Women talk today about having it all; well, Mom had it all back when I was a kid—all the responsibilities. With my father away so much, she had to administer the discipline, help us with our homework, sew our clothes, take care of the animals and garden, cook, and clean. And this was in a time and a place where very little was store-bought: housewives made their own soap and butchered their own livestock while the leather britches and apple butter were simmering away on the stove.

The woman who sat before me now in the wheelchair couldn't walk and, in the short time since I'd seen her last, had lost much of her ability to talk. She seemed to have trouble hearing, or maybe the problem was retaining her concentration.

I told her about the quilts I'd seen at Pansy's house and she said nothing, but she did smile. Her face was still smooth and clear under her fresh hairdo. And, a little while later, as she silently ate the food Pansy had prepared for us, I saw that her arms were still rounded and firm.

As I watched her, I thought about how our own household had mirrored the split personality of Lincoln County. On the one hand, you had my dad, Albert Hal Yeager, who liked to have a good time and went to church only because Mom dragged him. And on the other hand, there was Mom, who was the symbol of proper behavior for us Yeager kids.

Susie Mae and Hal had an interesting relationship, playing a kind of cat-and-mouse game that went on all their married lives. As the breadwinner, Dad was ostensibly the boss. And yet the house was run basically by Mom's rules—rules which I discovered you could bend but could never be broken without severe consequences. Even though she frowned on drinking, for example, Dad was allowed to dabble in brewing homemade blackberry wine. But as soon as dabblin' turned to outright drunkenness, as it did sometimes, Mom would go down to the basement and drop some camphor ice into Dad's fermenting vat and ruin his whole damn supply, just like that. The punishment was administered simply and cleanly. There'd be no threats beforehand or complaints afterward; nor would the incident ever be rehashed. She'd just go do it, and the case would be closed.

The curious thing was that although Mom won every battle that I can remember, she never succeeded in reforming Dad, who was always up for a little hell-raising, practically till the day he died. Glennis and I still laugh about how Mom used to go looking for Dad, saying, "Oh, no, he's gone down off the hill again."

For a brief second I wanted to share that memory with Mom, but then I looked into her eyes and I doubted that I could ever get through to her again with a complex thought. Sylvia must have read my mind.

"Your mom's getting tired from the excitement of having you here," she said. "I'll wheel her into her room for a while while Pansy and I do the dishes."

"Okay," I said, "I'll drive around a bit and check this old town out."

"Where you going?" she asked.

"Does Little Pete Browning still have his place?"

"I reckon," she replied. Then, thinking of the hospital-

75

ity at Browning's B&B Market, she quickly added, "But I don't see how you can eat anything after the candied sweet potatoes and butterscotch pie."

"Don't worry," I said, "I'm going on a fishing trip to Alaska next week and I probably won't eat till then."

The B&B Market is just off the main route between Hamlin and West Hamlin. A five-mile stretch of road separates the two towns, and on days when I didn't have too many chores to do, I used to walk it, barefoot, for no particular reason, just something to do. For provisions I'd take along a biscuit and a raw onion, which I'd eat as I sauntered along. That was enough for me to survive on. But sometimes I'd stop into Browning's B&B Market, which was run by ol' Big Pete then, to see what he had to offer. "Charles, what can I get you?" Mr. Browning would always holler. "A baloney sandwich?" It didn't matter if I didn't have the money right then. I could always pay him another time. Baloney wasn't his livelihood, anyway. Pete supplemented his income in a county where the only brew you could sell legally was that 3.2 dishwater, by bootlegging some honest-to-God beer.

Now, when I pulled up, there was an old bearded guy sitting out front with a CB radio in his lap, absentmindedly turning the dials. He looked at me kind of strangely as I went by, and I wondered if he recognized me—or if I should recognize him. I am something between a celebrity and a long-lost cousin to most folks around here. The big blue sign outside Hamlin says "Home of Charles E. Yeager, First Man to Fly Faster than Sound."

"Why, Charles Yeager," people will say when I'm back for a visit, as if they're part of my extended family. And that's fine. My only problem is remembering *them*. After all, it's been a long, long while since I moved out west with Glennis. Forty-odd years change people a lot.

76

But I didn't have any trouble remembering Little Pete Browning. If I hadn't recognized his face, now that he's even balder than I am, I'd have known him from his greeting. "Goddamn, how 'bout a ham sandwich, Charles?" he called from across the counter in the back of the store, while I was still up among the soda pop and potato chips. "How 'bout some nice barbecue? Comes from corn-fed beef."

I declined politely, telling him that I had dropped Pansy off at Mom's, had lunch there, and needed to get back. But I did take a tour of his meat freezer, at his insistence, and we reminisced a bit.

"Remember when my dad was a mite upset with you," Pete said, "because when you came buzzing over our little farm you knocked down all the corn in his field?"

"Yeah." I laughed, thinking of that time when I'd flown down to Hamlin with a P-47 from Wright Field in Dayton, Ohio. "And remember when I told him, 'Don't worry, Mr. Browning, I'll just fly out in the other direction and stand it all up again!' "

On the way back from the Brownings', I drove through Hamlin. The town which had a population of about 800 when I was a kid has grown to about 2000, not so much by sprawling as by becoming more dense. Instead of only one house per square block, there are now four or five houses on the same lot. With so much less space, people can no longer raise livestock or grow enough vegetables to support the household needs. That means—even though the McDonald'ses and the Pizza Huts haven't invaded Main Street yet—that the experience of living in Hamlin has changed fundamentally.

Mom's place—the house Dad built for them after the War—sits locked and shuttered. Just across the street, though, the big white house I was raised in is now home to another family. I stopped my car for a minute and took a look and thought of the coat of paint I'd put on just before I went off to the War. World War II, that is, but it was the only one we had around at the time, so everybody just called it the War. That old house still had a tin roof that makes for such a racket in a rain- or hailstorm. But the big strong oak tree I used to play in for countless hours as a kid—a tree that looked like it would live forever—had fallen over, and the people who lived there now had begun cutting it up for firewood.

OTHER VOICES

Glennis Yeager

Hamlin is a hard place to reach from the outside—in more ways than one. I mean it's *way* off the beaten track, back in the hills, the kind of town where even McDonald's hasn't put up their golden arches yet. But even if you find it, it's the kind of town that can be difficult to become a real part of unless you were born there.

Believe me, I know, because I tried.

The first time I went to West Virginia was to get married. It was a Methodist service, conducted in the Yeagers' home, and the reception was held in the high school gym where Chuck went to school.

When I went there to get married I was meeting his family for the first time, but I already knew them in a way. Chuck never said anything to me about marriage before he went overseas, but he had told his folks I was the one he was going to settle down with, I guess, because after he left for England I started getting letters from his mother. And, of course, I wrote back.

At first we were bucking each other up in a general sort of way, just by keeping in touch, the way so many families did in those days. But then his mother got word that Chuck had been shot down over France and was officially listed as missing in action. She called me up then and we both agreed, "If anyone can get through this, it's Charles." But in reality both of us didn't know what to think. I was not only anxious, I was confused, because I was his "sort-of" fiancée. We had both said we'd see other people during the time he was away and my feelings about him weren't fully sorted out yet.

His mother felt worried in a different sort of way. She had already lost a brother in World War I; his name was Richard and he'd been real handy with a gun, a fishing rod, and an ax, so he was one of Chuck's boyhood heroes. She wasn't over that yet by any means. Now that poor woman found herself waiting and worrying, deeply, the way only a mother can.

She was always a religious woman but now, suddenly, there was a lot about God and saying prayers in her letters. Later I found out that she lost more than thirty pounds during that period, which included a horrible false alarm when a local newspaper mistakenly reported Chuck as dead. I still have a clipping: *Yeager Killed*, the headline says. The War Department had called her and told her there'd been an error even before she read it. Still, it was torture for her. The whole time, though, I bet she never expressed a "poor me" thought because, as she might have said, "That's certainly not going to help mat-

79

ters any, is it?" That's just the way Chuck and his family are; they suffer in silence and seem devoid of self-pity.

The next time she called it was months later, to say that Chuck was safe in Spain. She was elated, as you might expect, but somehow scarred by that terrible suspense she had endured. I think the memory of that intense time stayed with her for years.

In 1945, when Chuck was back, I tried to live in West Virginia and make a go of it as a new bride; it was, in some ways, an exciting and happy time. The War was over, our men were home, and the future was ours for the making. So why wasn't I on cloud nine?

Well, for the simple reason that reality was quickly setting in. I suffered morning sickness all the time, because I was pregnant with our first child, Donald. Chuck was stationed at Wright Patterson Air Force Base in Dayton, Ohio, 160 miles away. And Chuck's mother had taken a job at a grocery store in Hamlin, as a clerk, partly to occupy her mind so she didn't keep reliving the War.

We had bought our first house, in Hamlin, but Chuck got home only on weekends and I was very lonely. I tried to make a go of it in that place all by myself, but that feeling of isolation persisted. Despite our mutual interest in Chuck, I still didn't know the other Yeagers that well, and I felt a little like a foreigner in a place where everyone had this heavy twang and used a lot of words and phrases that aren't in the English language. I just couldn't relate to their way of living. Everything about them seemed strange. I thought it was weird, for example, that they kept wallpapering their houses every few years, but that they always put one layer of paper on top of another until the walls were so thick and bumpity that it looked ridiculous. Then they'd pull it off and start again.

I also couldn't understand why the Republican Methodists went to the church up on the hill while the Democratic Methodists worshipped in the church "down in the holler." What did politics have to do with religion anyway? And why did these people, many of whom were getting the short end of the stick from politicians, feel so loyal to one party or another? Why, when Chuck's dad was introduced to Harry Truman (this was when Chuck got the Collier Award in 1948), ol' Hal Yeager actually refused to shake the President's hand. The Yeagers, who went to the up-on-the-hill church, just didn't "cotton to no Democrats nohow."

One day not long after we'd moved into our house in Hamlin, the people we'd bought it from came by and said they didn't like their new place, and would I consider selling them their old home back. I didn't have to think about it long. They got it back for what we had paid for it. I guess my "killer instinct" for real estate deals hadn't developed yet. Or maybe I was just feeling desperate to get out of what I saw as a depressing situation. In any case, I moved in with Chuck's mother and father and took over the cleaning and cooking because they were both off working most of the time. Pansy Lee was going through some kind of teenage phase at the time. She was rebelling against the household, and the only thing she'd work at was to make her own clothes. Of course, all women did that. For instance, in cutting up sugar and flour sack material for shirts and dresses, Chuck's mother was very particular about the brands she bought because some were made of finer material or were better colored than others. Mrs. Yeager did do beautiful stitching, but she was always growling about how "sloppy" or "loose," or "not right, just not right" everyone else's work was. She'd join a quilting party as long as it was someone else's quilt

81

they were working on. But her own she always made herself, start to finish.

It seemed like a large family. I was keeping house, cooking, and cleaning for Hal, Jr., Chuck's younger brother, Pansy Lee, older brother, Roy, some of the time, and the two older Yeagers, of course. Plus whoever showed up. There was a gang for supper every night. I don't know how much they enjoyed it, because I was a student-cook, learning with each meal. And one thing I learned was that I was not a great fan of West Virginia cuisine. The corn bread every night and the biscuits—made from scratch—every morning seemed monotonous to me. Their penchant for pouring hot pork grease over everything on their plates seemed downright strange. Heck, they even put those hot, greasy drippings on salad, and made what they call "wilted lettuce." Chuck would never eat that way now; I rarely cook red meat for him or let him have butter. Those things clog the arteries, and his brother Roy died of a heart attack that was no doubt hastened along by his diet. I don't worry about Chuck sticking to a good diet on the road either. I know he'll do it. He's never been one for fancy restaurants and foods with rich sauces. Besides, he quit drinking a long time ago, and he has taken up daily jogging and become a firm believer in good nutrition.

So while he hasn't changed in some ways, in other respects—in his approach to life-style, for instance—Chuck is right in tune with the times.

I have a unique perspective on Chuck. I'm the only one who has seen so clearly where he's come from and where he is today. And that a boy from Hamlin could wind up a hero to millions simply amazes me. Though I manage the "career" that has come about as a result of all this, I've really never gotten used to the idea.

Neither has Chuck. But rather than being impressed by all the attention he gets, he's amused, I think, that the world would want to celebrate and shower lucrative offers upon someone for a set of characteristics—resourcefulness, strength, peace of mind, and sometimes brutal honesty—that were so common among the poor anonymous folk of Hamlin.

───────────────────

Glennis could never adjust to the Lincoln County lifestyle. We tried it for a while when we first got married, even going so far as buying our own house and trying to become part of the community. When I wound up being transferred out west to Muroc to be a test pilot, we'd been living in Hamlin only a few months. But that's just as well, because I could tell by just looking at the expression on Glennis's face that the transplant wasn't going to take. She's a tough woman, raised on a Bangor, California, farm. But she could never get used to the shortage of farmable land back here in this rocky hill country, or to the lack of jobs that left many families barely able to survive. Then there were those unpredictable winter snows and those all-too-predictable springtime floods each year that drove the folks down by the Mud River from their tumbledown homes. Glennis once said to me as we drove down some poor excuse for a highway: "Life, Chuck, doesn't *have* to be this hard."

Now I know what she meant. But while I was growing up, I took the living conditions in my hometown for granted.

When I got back to Sylvia's place, Mom was sitting in

the living room—and so was a local sculptor who was working on a life-size statue of me that would stand outside Hamlin High School. The model figure he wanted to show me was about ten inches high; it showed me wearing a flight suit and a parachute on my back. I advised him on a few minor matters about the gear, so that the statue would be as authentic as possible. The whole while I spoke to him, Mom couldn't seem to take her eyes off that figure of me.

Then it was time to go. Mom obviously knew what was going on, but all she could manage to do was smile and say, "Charles." But that was enough, really. I didn't realize, then, that she wouldn't live to see the actual statue unveiled. But like I said, she understood what it was about, and that was what mattered.

When I said good-bye I didn't dwell on the idea that this might be our last parting or anything like that. My mother was clearly happy about Hamlin High School and the statue. She was well fed and comfortable and cared for, and she was not plagued by the usual pains of age. There was just the slow physical deterioration and now this rapid disconnection of her mind from what was happening around her. I could do nothing about the inevitable, but Pansy Lee had done right to call me: and now it was time to move on.

So for me this was just a happy parting. And that was as good as one could ask.

Pansy and I rode in silence for a while as I drove her back to Hurricane. I thought she probably felt the same way I did.

Presently, she glanced over at me and asked, "What are you thinking about?"

I smiled. I was thinking about pressing on.

"Oh, about making plane connections between Huntington and New Orleans," I said. "About a trip to Korea for Northrop and another trip to West Germany for the Air Force. And my buddy Andy and I are going to New Zealand on a trout-fishing expedition somewhere further along in there.

"For a retired guy, I'm gonna be having a very busy year."

4

THE GOLDEN
YEARS

In fact, the years have been busy ever since I took my first giant step into the "real world" when I joined the Army Air Corps in 1941. All I wanted to be back then was a mechanic helping on trucks, planes, heavy equipment— shoot, it didn't matter as long as it was hands-on experience with engines. But by chance I got caught up in a short-lived program that allowed enlisted men to fly. After that, some spectacular things happened to me—and fast. First I went west, to Tonopah, Nevada, to train as a fighter pilot. Then I found myself headed to a P-51 squadron in England. I flew my Mustang, the *Glamorous Glennis,* on many missions over France and Germany, got shot down, made my way back to England—and flew more missions in the *Glamorous Glen III.*

By the time the War was over I had a budding friendship going with a fellow fighter pilot named Bud Anderson, a native of Newcastle, California, whom I'd trained with at Tonopah, and flew with on two tours of duty. Besides, Glennis—still my fiancée at that point—happened to live just up the road from Andy, as I call him, in Oroville. So instead of going back to West Virginia, I arranged to have myself sent to California, and though I've been moved around a lot by the Air Force over the years—going everywhere from Texas to West Germany, Pakistan and Vietnam—California was where I most often stayed. It's where my children were raised for the most part, and it was where, as a test pilot, I worked on numerous research projects, most notably the X-1, the aircraft that first successfully broke the sound barrier in a controlled experiment, making me the first man to fly faster than the speed of sound.

I retired from the Air Force as a brigadier general in 1975, but it seems I didn't retire from anything else. I'm busier now than ever—consulting for the U.S. government and for private aircraft manufacturers, making TV commercials for AC Delco and other companies, and giving speeches.

I've had to face up to the fact that my plans to become just another anonymous army mechanic have pretty much gone to hell. Without ever applying for the position, it seems I've become a hero.

That's very flattering, of course, but it's also something to contend with in this day and age—one of the most dangerous "missions," you might say, that I've ever been on. Why? Because to be a hero in the late 1980s means that lots of people want a part of you. And if you're not careful you can, in a sense, lose your life to the demands of fame.

The requests to speak, to endorse, to appear on this podium or at that dinner, come in daily by telephone and mail to my home. Usually the answer is no, because I'm booked solid for a year in advance. Things have gotten so hectic that Glennis and I have found it necessary to hire a secretary, Cindy Siegfried, to help answer the mail and handle the phones. Oh, yeah, I'm retired all right. But if I wanted to, I could be working 365 days a year.

I want to make it clear that I'm not complaining about all these opportunities, or about the way my retirement has turned out. Hell, I'm the type that gets restless sitting around for very long—like an hour or two. I enjoy being on the go, meeting people, sharing what I've learned about life—and yes, earning the big bucks that go with these offers, so I can pass it along to my kids and grandkids. Still, my point about "losing your life" is this: if you say "yes" to too many offers, you can wake up one morning in another fancy hotel room and realize that you're not really living, you're just making personal appearances.

That's not the way I want to live. And so a few years ago, when what I call "the hero business" suddenly got to be altogether too much, Glennis became my business manager, the chief executive officer of Yeager, Inc., a kind of kitchen-table corporation we set up to deal with my business affairs.

Hell, I'm probably one of the first guys from Hamlin ever to *have* any business affairs.

<hr>

OTHER VOICES

Glennis Yeager

There were just the two of us, my sister and I, but we grew up thinking that it didn't matter that we were girls— there wasn't anything we couldn't accomplish if we set our minds to it. My father was the big influence in this regard. One of my earliest memories is of him digging a well in back of our house. That well was ninety feet deep and he did it all by himself, first digging down through thirty feet of soil, then, when he reached hard rock, drilling holes and putting dynamite in and blasting. Each step in this huge undertaking required that he go down a ladder and haul out the loose dirt and gravel, bucket by bucket, dumping it into a wheelbarrow and carting it away. Anyone who's seen a man sink his own well in the Butte County soil understands that there's no job too big if you've got the gumption. (He let me get in the bucket one day and windlassed me all the way to the bottom— I'll never forget seeing stars at noon.)

That kind of background toughened me up, and so as I got older I was never surprised when I hit a rough patch in life's road. As kids growing up during the Depression, we had to do our own work around my family's little ranch. Burning out tree stumps from a field—now that may have been the hardest task I ever faced. I was only about ten and some of those stumps were as green as I was, and so they just wouldn't burn or budge no matter how much you hacked at the roots. My father was paying me ten cents a stump, though, and besides, they just *had* to get removed so he could plow the field and plant wheat for our horse and our milk cow. Somehow or other, just by hanging in there, and as Chuck would say, "pressing on," I got the job done.

All that hard work never turned me into a tomboy though. I always wore dresses to school and had a good sense of color and proportion and was interested in being feminine. But I just don't think there's a contradiction between being strong and being a lady. That's something my mother could never see. She wanted to be a lady so bad that she didn't ever want to get her fingernails dirty or her hair mussed up or anything like that. And it's because she was raised that way. She was very tiny and looked delicate. She'd been a premature baby, raised by her grandmother, and they just treated her like a little china doll. They used to decorate her, do her hair in curls, dress her up. She was a doll all her life—a plaything. But underneath it all she was really tenacious and willful. Maybe I'm a bit like that myself. I loved her, but I used the way she behaved as an example of something I didn't want to be. I guess you could say, in the language of today, that I wanted it all. I wanted to be able to shoot a gun, fix a car, run an office—and attract men too. And that's the way it worked out. I think one thing Chuck liked about me from the start was that he could talk to me without feeling he was talking to a pretty moron.

And maybe our both being strong has meant that we've had our problems. I can recall one time, back in the late '40s, we were in Cincinnati and I got so fed up with Chuck, I scooped up our son Don and hopped a flight for San Diego, where my parents were living at the time. I was a complete wreck—so upset that I left my purse in an airport phone booth and once we were airborne I had to ask the pilot to radio back to Cincinnati. He did, and the security guard went and found the purse and put it on another plane and it actually beat me to California. I remember all that very clearly, and I remember feeling that was *it*, the Air Force could keep this guy as far as I was concerned—but I'll be darned if I can remember what caused that big blowup in the first place other than built-up frustration over trying to take care of a six-month-old baby while being moved from one place to another every few weeks.

Chuck has forgotten the whole incident. I know because

I reminded him of it recently and he just looked at me like I was some crazy person making it all up.

It's not that he's insensitive. He knew how hard it was to make ends meet on that 1946 Air Force paycheck, and he realized that being constantly uprooted (and set down somewhere else on a "temporary duty" basis, which precluded us from getting convenient quarters at the base) was certainly no piece of cake. But he also knew that there was no use worrying about something he was powerless to control, so nothing about military life ever stuck in his craw. When you tallied up the score, he was having a grand ol' time flying planes, and that offset the hardships. End of discussion.

What ultimately happened, though, as far as our "separation" is concerned, was that he borrowed a car and drove all the way out to California to get me. He never called, he just showed up one day at my parents' house about two weeks later. And I never demanded an apology or offered one of my own. I just got into the car with the baby and went back with him and we never said another word about it.

The more I look around at other people, especially young people, and see what happens to their marriages, the more I realize Chuck and I had a special relationship.

———————————————

Glennis to this day maintains that back before the War when I first walked into the USO office out in Oroville, California, where she worked, and started to talk to her about arranging a dance for the guys in my squadron, she could hardly understand what I was saying. My Lincoln

County drawl was part of the problem, she maintains, but there was also this whole other set of words I had—"poke" for paper sack, "turned like" for resembles—that kept her off balance. She says she'd never seen such an out-and-out hillbilly except in the movies. Perhaps. But when I told her, "You can get girls for all my buddies, but *you're* going to this dance with me tonight," she seemed to understand me all right, and she went as my date and we both had a good time.

I was flattered that she even went with me. After all, she wasn't someone who'd be impressed with a guy just because he was wearing a uniform, the way a lot of girls were in those staunchly patriotic times. No, Glennis was a level-headed girl who worked every evening in that USO office (as well as holding down two other jobs). She was surrounded by soldiers all the time and surely the novelty had worn off. She also knew enough about how things worked in the military to realize that if I was coming in to set up a dance, that meant I was the low man on the totem pole. Still, about a week later she went out with me again, to a picnic. I got to know her a little better there and found out that she was raised on a farm and that she liked hunting and fishing and that was it; from that day forward we were a team as far as I was concerned.

(It wasn't until after the War that I would find out just how good an outdoorswoman Glennis was—a crack shot with a rifle like no other woman I've ever seen. While we were stationed in Germany in the early '50s, she amazed everyone with her ability to shoot skeet with the best marksmen at the Rod and Gun Club. What's more, virtually all of the hunting trophies, the red stag, elk, and roebuck horns that hang on our living room walls in Grass Valley, come from animals that Glennis harvested while we were stationed there.)

Glennis and I agree on at least one point about our whirlwind courtship: I never actually asked her to marry me. But when I was sent to England to join the War over Europe in 1943, I was straightforward enough, in my West Virginia fashion, to simply start sending her part of my paycheck, telling her to put this in an account for us.

When we actually tied the knot after the War, our wedding was held in my parents' house, with the reception at the local high school. There was a little band there, just for listening I guess, because when Glennis and I got up to foxtrot, you should have seen the shocked looks we got from some of the churchgoing folk in the community. Their reaction made me think of a certain downhome saying: the people of Lincoln County never make love standing up—because somebody might think they're dancing. Just the same, Glennis and I agreed to try and make Hamlin our home base.

After our wedding we went to an army rest and recreation facility for a couple of weeks in Santa Monica, California. We put on our swimsuits, walked out onto the beach, and, to our delighted astonishment, ran right into Bud Anderson and his new wife, Eleanor. We hadn't even known they were engaged! They had married three days before us. Theirs is kind of an unusual story, one of many, I suppose, brought about by the War. Ellie had been married for a few months to Bud's boyhood friend, Jack Stacker, a P-38 fighter pilot who was shot down and killed over Europe. Though they had gone to the same high school in Auburn, California, she hardly even knew Bud—until he started writing her from overseas. In any case, seeing them there was quite a surprise, and ever since, Andy and I have taken a lot of kidding about how we were so close we even went on our honeymoon together.

Pretty soon after that, however, I couldn't help but

experience the kind of letdown I guess almost every pilot had after coming back from the War. After all, combat in many ways was the ultimate assignment for any pilot. In the '40s, with the whole country swept up in the War effort, we fighter pilots were on the front lines, the glamorous stars of the ultimate show, and we gloried in our status. Shooting down German planes was both our job and our reward, all rolled up in one. Nothing else mattered to us. I wasn't the only flier who felt like that. All of the better pilots, the aggressive guys, will tell you that though it's a deadly game you're playing—and perhaps *because* of that—combat is a "high."

So after the War my quest for constant excitement led me to getting involved in air shows for a little while in the '40s. Some other Air Force pilots and myself would get in our jet fighters and put on a show for some local civic or social group by buzzing down Main Street and doing some aerial acrobatics. It was a thrill for the people who were watching because jet planes were brand new at the time and you could draw a crowd just by taxiing around in something that didn't have a propeller. It was good for the pilot's ego, too, because with the War fresh in everybody's memory, those of us stunt fliers who'd been successful in combat would get our share of praise. But the thrill didn't last long for me. Without some Germans trying to wax my fanny in a dogfight, flying around doing stunts quickly became a dull afternoon's work, and I realized the air shows would not provide the adrenaline fix I was after.

The X-1 project, on the other hand, certainly would. Although it meant working in California at a time when my growing family was just getting started in West Virginia, getting involved in the project to reach Mach 1 was something I desperately wanted to do. For one thing, the then-controversial question of whether man could fly faster than the speed of sound excited my natural curiosity. I knew that the speed of sound was 760 mph at sea level, and 660 mph at 40,000 feet. Flying Mustangs in the War, I'd experienced the shock waves that slammed against my ailerons and stabilizer when I'd exceeded 500 mph in a steep power dive. At that speed, the turbulent air traveling over the curved upper surface of my wing had, for brief intervals, actually exceeded the speed of sound—and caused tremendous buffeting that could pull the plane apart. "Compressibility," this was called, and because of it many scientists held fast to the theory of an actual sound barrier that would destroy any airplane that attempted to crash through the invisible wall. In early 1947, Geoffrey De Havilland, Jr., a British test pilot, had been blown to pieces at .94 Mach, when his tailless experimental plane disintegrated. It was hard to look at all the evidence and then just dismiss what they called a "brick wall in the sky" at 660 mph.

I felt that the whole subject was beyond my understanding when, on a quick chance visit to Muroc in 1946, I first saw the X-1—a small orange, rocket-propelled ship. Still, in the back of my mind, I suspected—despite my experiences in the Mustang and in an early jet fighter, the P-84 Thunderjet that shook violently and pitched up at .82 Mach—that there was no "invisible wall" at Mach 1. I knew the engineers and the rocket scientists who thought otherwise were making highly educated guesses based on years of study and tons of data. But I had some experience of my own, in the backwoods of West Virginia. I knew that a bullet traveled faster than the speed of sound without coming apart at the seams. So, I reasoned, why the hell couldn't a properly designed airplane? Of course,

I wasn't absolutely sure I was correct, and the whole X-1 project was so complex that there were hundreds of things that could have gone disastrously wrong as we tried to slip past Mach 1. Yet some letters that I wrote Andy around that time, and which he recently discovered, show that I was pretty confident. "Don't sweat this deal," I told him. And though the X-1 development was highly classified, and I couldn't discuss it with even my best friend, I added, "We're gonna meet our goals on this project in due time."

Looking back, I was more anxious about getting assigned to the project than about breaking the sound barrier. The Air Force had started work on the project with a civilian test pilot named Slick Goodlin, but the deal fell through when Goodlin demanded a $150,000 bonus if and when he reached Mach 1. Once I'd heard that the Air Force was switching to a military pilot, I applied for the job of making that historic flight. At first I thought I had no shot at the X-1; they were looking for an unmarried guy because of the danger involved, and besides, I didn't think I had enough seniority to get it. So after I put my name on the list, I really didn't think about it. But when I realized I was in the running, and I went with Bob Hoover (my eventual backup pilot) and Jack Ridley (my flight engineer) to check out the orange monster at the Bell Aircraft plant in Buffalo, New York—hell, I positively salivated at the thought of punching a hole in the sound barrier. I'd finally found an assignment that would keep me on the ragged edge, where I was naturally most comfortable.

"This is highly dangerous work," Colonel Albert Boyd, head of the flight test division at Wright Field, reminded me, rather unnecessarily, when he called me in to tell me I had the X-1 assignment. I kept a sober expression as he spoke, or tried to, but all I could think was, "What a deal!" Yes, here was the answer to my postwar blues.

The X-1 project wound up taking about seven months to complete. After eight powered flights, during which that little orange monster was dropped from the belly of a B-29 bomber at 20,000 feet, we reached Mach 1 on October 14, 1947. In the end, what was most memorable about that historic flight was what didn't happen. We didn't disintegrate, didn't "hit the wall," didn't even feel a bump when we went supersonic. We just sailed along like that bullet that I knew could produce a minisonic boom, right into the pages of aviation history.

On that fall day in '47, though, I was not exactly transformed into an instant hero; Glennis picked me up in our car, as usual, and I flopped in, real beat. If Dick Frost and Bob Hoover hadn't come over to congratulate me, she wouldn't have known what I'd done that day. The news had to be kept classified by the Air Force for nine months so that American scientists could complete and digest the data. Nobody said we couldn't celebrate though. And so a bunch of the guys from Muroc went out to Pancho's place that night, our steady drinking hangout there in the desert, and we really tied one on. But the next day it was back to business as usual, hung over but happy to know that eventually we'd be part of aviation history. Then we simply moved along to the next challenge—testing the landing gear of the X-1 and checking out the bumper crop of new jets that were pouring in for us to test-fly. This was the golden age of military aviation and I was as happy as a pig in slop, hopping in and out of as many as twenty-seven different kinds of airplanes in some months.

So test-piloting was my work, and the nearby Sierras my playground. It was a perfectly balanced life for a guy like me, who enjoys working hard and playing even harder.

I was stationed at Muroc, which eventually became Edwards Air Force Base, from 1947 to 1948, and again from 1949 to 1954. Most of the time I worked a five-day week, pushing "the outside of the envelope," as research fliers say, for eight hours a day at a salary of around $500 a month. I'd leave our two-room adobe "house" (Glennis had given up on Hamlin and joined me despite the miserable living conditions) at about seven each morning, make the twenty-six-mile drive to the base—and arrive home in the evening just in time to eat dinner. Often, after I became famous for breaking the sound barrier, there'd be speaking engagements that took me out of town until the next morning. This didn't give me much time with my family, but I didn't fret about that because fretting wouldn't have given me any more hours in the day or otherwise changed the way things worked out. The simple fact of the matter was that I had a job to do, and if I was going to do it right, I needed not just the time I spent at the base but some additional time to unwind and recover. Glennis understood that, and the kids took their lead from her.

Glennis fully understood this need of mine to let off steam and have fun; she knew that unless I did I couldn't do my job right, and so there were never any questions asked. I can remember being off giving a talk somewhere and not having a jet airplane at my disposal so I was flying commercial, which in those days meant that I flew into Los Angeles. That night I got in at about eleven P.M. and Glennis picked me up and drove me home. It was about three A.M. when we reached the house—and there, sitting in the driveway, is my old friend Bob Uhrig, a maintenance officer at Edwards.

"Hey, c'mon," he runs up and says to me, "we're going fishing in Idaho in the middle fork of the Salmon River.

We called ahead and got horses hired and all the guys are ready to go."

Well, I looked at Glennis and didn't have to say anything.

"Go ahead if you want," she said. And it was as simple as that with her. She wasn't being a martyr or anything; she meant it: if it makes you happy, go.

What a trip that turned out to be. I remember running into my house in the middle of the night and grabbing my fishing gear, and the next thing I knew I was with six other guys on a C-47, and we were winging our way toward Idaho. We landed in a big field, and a friend of ours, Gus Julian, picked us up in a couple of trucks and took us to where the horses were.

Riding was no big deal to most of us, but one guy, Tony Padavitch, had never been in a saddle. He was always lagging behind, probably because he was scared out of his wits and had his horse reined in so tightly. But of course the animal wouldn't abide that for very long; he'd get lonesome for his friends up ahead and take off. And here'd come old Tony, with all these pots and pans he'd tied on all over the horse, going clank, clankity, clank, and yelling, "Whoa, horsey, whoa, horsey."

We didn't have sleeping bags or tents with us; the trip had been such a spur-of-the-moment thing that all we had was some canvas cloth to lie on, some cooking utensils, and booze. We spent two nights down there on the Salmon River and we were so keyed up from our week of test-piloting that I don't think we got one bit of sleep. We just caught fish, built a big fire, and sat around it all night bullshitting.

On Sunday, when we had to get back to Edwards, I was more tired than I've ever been in my life. Still, I insisted, as I usually do when I'm with a group of pilots, on flying the plane. And I can remember sitting there in that Gooney Bird, looking into the sun—and falling sound asleep. The plane was on auto pilot, but pretty soon some joker would come up behind me and drop a big toolbox on the floor from a height of about three feet.

Boom!

I'd wake up in stark terror, then drift off to sleep again a few minutes later.

How we made it back to Edwards alive I still don't know.

And yet that wasn't the end of the line for me. I had to leave California that same night in an F-86 and go east to Patuxent River, Maryland, to give another talk at the Navy Test Pilot School there. Glennis helped me pack and drove me back to the base for what we call a short-haul flight. In other words, I didn't have any drop tanks on that F-86 and so I'd go from Edwards to Albuquerque, Albuquerque to Oklahoma City, from there to St. Louis, and so on. There was no high altitude mandatory traffic control in those days, and so I'd fly all night talking only to the airfield control towers for takeoff and landings.

When I finally got to Patuxent, I gave my speech and turned right around and headed back. I remember being up there at around 42,000 feet and falling asleep again. Except there was no one to drop any toolbox then; I was all alone. In that situation I'd just stay sleeping until I felt the airplane diving or heard a change in the drone of the engine. Then I'd wake up again—for a while.

In its own way, the golden age was as thrilling as aerial combat—and at times it was just as dangerous. I came as close as I ever got to "buying the farm" during a 1953 flight in the X-1A, a high-speed, high-altitude craft that was meant to pick up where the X-1 had left off. It was my fault. Because the sun blinded me for an interval as I

101

climbed into the desert sky, I found myself flying too high, too fast. I was up to about 80,000 feet—so high I could see stars in the daytime sky—and traveling at 2.3 Mach when I realized that the atmosphere was too thin to support my aircraft, and I was totally out of control. Within moments I was spinning around the sky in four different directions at once, and, despite my safety harness, getting battered in the canopy within an inch of my life. It looked hopeless. The ground was coming up at me at the rate of 1,000 feet per second, and nothing I tried seemed to work. I still don't know how I pulled out of it, but at about 25,000 feet I did and managed to land only a little bumpily on Rogers Dry Lake bed. When I got home, Glennis saw that I was pale and shaken and that my eyes were bloodshot from pulling heavy Gs. I had a speaking commitment that night at a fancy dinner in Los Angeles, an hour and a half drive from our house. Glennis thought we should cancel out, but I said hell no, the best thing to do would be to just press on. If we sat around for too long thinking about what had happened that day, I might never want to get in an airplane again. As usual, Glennis understood. Within the limits of doing whatever really *had* to be done, each of us, I think, has always tried to let the other do whatever it was they *wanted* to do. Glennis has always been an independent person, running her own part of our lives together and understanding the pressures on me.

The golden age was a time when all-out flying meant all-out unwinding too. Often, of a Friday evening, four or five guys would get really fired up at Pancho's place. Then we'd hightail it into the High Sierras with our guns and fishing gear, totally forgetting about real-life responsibilities—and sometimes even our goddamn tents. The next couple of nights would be spent among the rattlesnakes and bears, getting hung over, rained on, bug-bit, and strung out from lack of sleep. In a way it was downright dumb. I mean, what if, after all that time and energy spent on successfully doing battle with the Luftwaffe, I had gone out and plowed into some California redwood tree? That kind of thing happened all the time to guys we knew, but we still didn't care. We thought we'd go on forever in those days, drinking like fish and driving like demons. And if we were wrong, hell, we didn't care about that either.

We were incapable of embarrassment. I remember one night, when we were heading up through Bakersfield on one of our weekend expeditions, passing a bottle around in the car and getting a little beyond the pale. "Let's stop up ahead," said Sid Smith, a lieutenant colonel who was deputy operations officer at Edwards, "there's a pretty park up here somewhere. Real remote. We can get some sleep there and head on in the morning."

We were in no shape to argue. And it was so dark we just stopped right there, got out our sleeping bags, took off our clothes, and climbed in.

Fade-out, fade-in to about 7:30 the next morning. The sun is shining. The birds are chirping. And there are about twenty people standing there at a bus stop a few feet from us, looking at these four hung-over bodies lying half out of their sleeping bags. I remember looking up at all those strange faces and thinking, "What the hell . . ."

Needless to say, we weren't in any remote area. We had camped out in the village square of this little town that was starting to go about its daily business. I'll never forget the couple of old ladies who were waiting for the bus while we, only a few feet away, floundered around, trying to get our clothes on.

That's one place where the folks know that Chuck Yeager puts on his pants one leg at a time.

Each weekend during that time was really a minivacation, a chance to escape the atmosphere of combined discipline and stress. I remember one year when deer season was about to open on a Saturday morning and a bunch of other test pilots and I were champing at the bit to get up to a favorite spot of ours around the town of Lee Vining, California, and do some hunting. My only problem was that I had a speaking engagement and couldn't get rolling until late Friday evening. "Why don't you guys head on up and get a campsite," I told the guys, "and me and Bob Uhrig will start out a few hours later and find you."

We decided that the first bunch would bring just what they needed for the night. Then Bob Uhrig (a real rounder) and I would haul up most of the equipment and food in a little swivel-wheel trailer that I'd made.

Those speechifying functions always go on longer than they should, with about three more speakers than the average person can tolerate, and so we got out late and were trying to make up for lost time. I had this big old Pontiac sedan, and we were hitting those curves at about seventy mph. I'd look back and see that trailer swinging wildly on its one wheel, this way and that, all over the road. But then things really got rough as we hit this rocky road that led to the campsite. Now, when we glanced back, we could see that trailer bouncing high each time we hit what turned out to be a series of big boulders. Never stopping, we pressed on.

At about three in the morning, and after driving along slowly for a while, we finally saw dim coals from a campfire. I pulled up and we heard this kind of drunken snoring coming through the darkness. "Well, here's their camp," I said to Uhrig. And then we did what any mature Air Force officers would have done in a similar situation: we pulled out all the tent pegs and laughed like hell while everybody flailed around under the canvas. Maybe they were tired, but we were still wound up from our trip.

"Everybody up," I said. "It's time for a hearty breakfast."

Predawn cocktails came first. Then we broke out our gasoline stove, got the skillet out, and I went to the trailer and pulled out our eggs—which, as it turned out, had not taken the trip in that trailer of mine very well. Not only were they scrambled, but quarter-inch pieces of shell were floating around in the container.

I poured the whole thing into one pan. Then I reached down and picked up a big handful of eggs in an attempt to filter the shells through my fingers. Needless to say, that didn't work very well.

You change as you get older. If you're like me, you all but quit drinking, you make sure you eat and sleep right, and generally lose interest in raising hell.

At the time, though, sitting there in the four A.M. darkness, and crunching on those hand-filtered scrambled eggs, it really seemed like a perfectly reasonable thing to do.

OTHER VOICES

Glennis Yeager

Everybody always says, gee, what a hard life it was, and when I look back on it, at the time, yes, I worked real hard and often was very tired and had four kids and did it all by myself and all that. Sure. But I didn't know that wasn't what I was supposed to be doing anyway. I mean, it wasn't as though I wanted to be doing anything else. I guess you could say I just didn't know any better.

You have to remember that at first it was still wartime. There had been a number of years of war when nothing was being built but airplanes and ships and weapons. There were no new cars and no new refrigerators, no housing, no air-conditioning—you name it, we didn't have it. I didn't even have a washing machine until I had my third baby. Being in the military was a way of life. This was a role I had chosen for myself, and I had this thing all through life that you finish what you start.

In a way, having to work so hard from day to day just to keep warm and fed and clean may have been a help in keeping me from worrying about Chuck. Although he always said, anytime I did start fretting, "Well, don't forget I'm in the plane too." In other words, relax; in research flying the pilot is not going to do anything deliberately foolish. I never could accept that really from other pilots, but I did learn to accept it from Chuck.

If you've ever seen the movie *The Right Stuff*, and you remember those scenes of Sam Shepard, playing Chuck, and Barbara Hershey, as me, exchanging steamy looks— well, our exact words may have been different in real life, but the basic message about us is absolutely true. We felt very strongly about each other because each of us had just what the other had been looking for, and I mean not just from the time we'd reached marriageable age, but all our lives. It's like we were *raised* for each other. Chuck was always independent, a man's man. He came from a household where his father was away six days a week, drilling for natural gas in the West Virginia hills. It was deeply ingrained in him that you could be a father and husband and not be around all the time.

And, sure enough, that's the way he lived his life. All

those years we were stationed at Edwards, he'd be off test-piloting airplanes five days a week—then on Friday night he and his friends would often head off into the hills for a weekend of hunting and fishing.

Meanwhile, I was raising four kids, washing diapers in the bathtub, putting on extra layers of clothing when the desert night wind would come whipping through our un-insulated bungalow—and generally feeling pretty good about it all. Why? Because, as I mentioned earlier, my mother presented an image of herself as physically and emotionally fragile—and I never liked that. It bothered me that my father had to do a lot of what I considered women's work. Early on I said to myself, if I get married, *my* home will never be like this. My husband would have to be someone who would give me the room to show I was independent and strong. The last thing I wanted was some sappy, clinging type of man—and certainly no one could ever accuse Chuck of being *that*. Although actually he was a real softie with our girls, whenever he was around. Chuck had very little time to spend with his family when the kids, Don, Mike, Sharon, and Susie, were real small. But when he was there, he was great. And always in a nitty-gritty situation, you could count on Chuck.

When I got so sick with the fourth pregnancy—that was Susie—he was terribly concerned; he was right there. He went out of his way to make sure I got the most care you could get. Same thing a few years ago when I first developed cancer—whatever he *could* do, he did. I never heard a word of worry from him and learned only later, from friends, how much he had fretted when I was having surgery and chemotherapy and so on. All I heard from him was the positive view, all I knew was his willingness to support someone making a fight for it. Well, he's always liked a fighter, and I guess that's another good reason we're well matched.

The fact is, in our growing up years—and heaven knows we were young enough ourselves to do a lot of growing up together—our roles were pretty sharply defined by the natural demands that four young kids, each roughly a year apart, make on the parent who is home. Chuck was the breadwinner, and I did everything else. Then, as the kids themselves got older, I had to find things to interest me. You could go crazy just taking care of four kids with no adults to talk to—and you could go crazy with some of the yack-yack stuff the adults came up with too. After Susie was born I took up bridge in a big way, eventually played duplicate and team play, and got into some very competitive playing. Then a little later, the kids might have been from three to seven, I taught swimming, first aid, life saving, and other things like that. I could have a couple of the kids with me at the officers' club and pool, working with me, and stash the ones I wasn't working with at the nursery just down the street. That was later, of course. Even later than that they wanted to learn how to bowl, so I went down to San Bernardino and took bowling instructions and became a certified instructor. This was really funny, because I was never a good bowler, but I was a real good teacher.

When it all got boring I took up golf and then decided to get into buying real estate. You know, it was just one thing or another, whatever turned me on at the time.

Finally the kids got out of the nest, and in time grew up to have their own families. Don, our eldest, lives in Colorado. He's a rancher and mason, does designs for chimneys and special rock walls and such. He married Frances Snyder and they have five kids. Mike, Michael, that is, he's a master sergeant in the Air Force and he's a pretty talented artist as well. He's married to Linda and they have three kids. Of course, being Air Force, they're bucketed about from one place to another. Our oldest girl, Sharon, is married to Stephen Flick and they have a place near here outside Reno. They also have three youngsters. And Susie Yeager Finnegan, our youngest, has two children, and they live right near here in Nevada City. The grandchildren seem to keep on coming. Chuck really enjoys their company, in reasonable doses, and certainly he's effective as a grandpa.

Our own kids—although they aren't kids anymore, of course—take their famous father in stride. They get a kick out of it but it has not affected them, really. Don, for instance—they'd just had a new baby and I was back there helping out, and whenever Chuck came on the TV with one of his commercials, Don would just sit there and crack up, laughing. None of them has ever made a big thing of having Chuck Yeager as a father, not as far as the fame is concerned anyway.

As for myself, as soon as the family was out of my hair, I went to work. When we went to the Philippines they had a real need for Red Cross volunteers, so I went to work as a Red Cross volunteer and continued on doing that wherever we were until we retired.

The thing is, I'd much rather be doing those things than going to hen parties, as I called them. I am not a good listener to yack. But working at the hospital let me out of a lot of boring social chitchat. And a couple of times, when Chuck got a bit more rank, I just flat out refused to feed visiting firemen when the commanding officer's wife told me to do so. She had the funds to do it, it was her job. She was just trying to slough it off on colonels' wives. Chuck backed me up. And another time was in Pakistan. The embassy people there, all they did, day and night, month in month out, was entertain around the different embassies. When I got there I said, wait a minute, I'm not doing this. And the thing was, within a week after you got there you were supposed to give a tea at your house to introduce yourself to all the embassy wives. That was protocol. Well, I thought that was for the birds, and I didn't do it. So the calls started coming—from the third in command, and the second in command—the wives, that is—and I'd say, "I'm not ready to give a tea." And then, "When I get ready, I'll give it." But finally, "*If* I get ready I may give it—and I think that's very doubtful." Well, it went straight up. But it just so happened that the ambassador and Chuck both backed me. Chuck said that protocol was a bunch of b.s. anyway. And I just didn't do it.

But when it came to two or three receptions a year that were required of Chuck, I did them. That was part of his job, so it was part of mine. But that's all I did. Because shortly after I got there I went to work for USAID in the embassy and ceased to get "yack" invitations. Which is what I wanted.

This was the first work for pay that I'd done since before we got married. It really felt good. Everything else had been volunteer, and I'd enjoyed it, but it doesn't really leave you feeling like grown-up people. . . .

I have been very, I guess the word is selfish, in a lot of ways. I did what I wanted to do and not what somebody else wanted me to do. I worked really hard for squadron luncheons and things like that—it was a lot of fun putting on shows and so on—but I never felt it was necessary to be bored for the sake of Chuck's career. And he wouldn't have wanted that either.

The truth is he really did need me, for all sorts of reasons, long before he became famous the way he is today. I always handled the finances, as meager as they might be, starting from before we were married when he used to send me half of his military pay each month from Europe. Even today I don't think he could begin to balance a checkbook. But I always handled all that, and managed to put away a little and eventually moved into some modest real estate investments that paid off handsomely. I bought several acres of land in Nevada County for $700 an acre—and sold it for $5000 an acre in 1976. Then I reinvested some of that in rental properties that panned out pretty well. I never had any formal training in real estate or accounting or any of the business managing I do now for Chuck. I learned a lot simply by reading, by watching others, and by applying some good common sense.

Maybe what makes Glennis so good at running Yeager, Inc., is the good head she carries. But what really sets her apart from any good New York City agent is that, like me, she's not seriously in it for the money. She's in it because it interests her—I mean it's a challenging function. She understands that my main objective for getting involved in a project is, does this thing sound like it might be some fun? Or, if I go there to make that speech, is there something else in that neck of the woods that it would be fun to do?

It's a simple idea—putting enjoyment before profit or glory—and one that I've clung to all my working life. But it seems to confuse the hell out of some of the more high-powered callers who reach us in Grass Valley. For example, a few years ago, when they were having that centennial for the Statue of Liberty in New York, Lee Iacocca's people contacted us about my leading a fly-by of World War II fighter planes as part of the celebration. They had their plans all laid out; I was supposed to swing by the statue in my P-51 with music playing and fireworks going off—and they just kind of assumed I'd go along with it all. But they hadn't checked with Glennis, who gave them a flat no. "Chuck will be fishing in the High Sierras on that day," she said, "and nothing interferes with that annual trip." Iacocca's people were flabbergasted, I'm sure, to be turned down in favor of some golden trout. But Glennis just figured, well, if they don't understand what we're all about, then that's their problem.

Of course many of my trips have taken me a helluva lot farther than the Sierras—but that's another story.

5

A LONG TRAMP OFF THE BEATEN TRACK

Bud Anderson

You are walking in a world that is strangely wet and dark. Tall trees form a canopy over you as you hike through the bush near the Ruakituri River on New Zealand's North Island. It is February—late summer in that part of the world and a season when the clouds are usually heavy with rain. And yet despite the constantly somber skies, there is nothing gloomy about the atmosphere on this fishing expedition—not as long as the colorful native birds called fantails flirt close to you as you trudge through the deep ferns, and my old friend Yeager brings up the rear.

"You know, Andy," Chuck calls out at one point, after we'd been making slow but steady progress over terrain that was strewn with vines and studded with mossy rocks,

"I've been following you for about five hours today, and I've noticed one thing."

"What's that, Chuck?"

(Pause while we skitter through a little stream.)

"You've got a goddamn droopy old-man's butt."

I take Chuck's remark in stride and wait for the chuckles from our two guides, Jerry and Keith, to subside.

"Well," I finally say, shooing a few sand flies from in front of my face as we proceed, "we've been dragging our butts over mountains and through rivers as a team for more than forty years now—so your butt can't be in much better shape than mine."

And we march on.

You kind of fall into a groove on one of these long hikes (or, to use the local argot, "tramps")—and your mind goes on automatic pilot.

Which is why we don't break stride when, after an hour of making our way up some rather steep and densely overgrown slopes, we suddenly find ourselves facing a yawning dry ravine. A large dead log has fallen across the gulch, forming a natural bridge. The log is a little rotten and covered with damp moss. Not the best footing, but no big deal either, even to a couple of senior citizens like Chuck and me. We're used to scampering across logs to cross fast-moving streams in the California High Sierras.

Keith goes across first. I follow him with no problem. Then, just as I'm about to step off onto solid ground, I hear a muffled exclamation and a sickening thud—the sound of a heavy sack hitting damp earth.

Except it isn't a heavy sack. It's Yeager.

Chuck has slipped and is lying at the bottom of the ravine, about twenty feet below. I can see that he has managed to twist around in midair and land on his back, so that the pack has apparently broken his fall. Still, he is sprawled there awkwardly on the sand, with a grimace frozen on his face. But no cusses are forthcoming; he is strangely silent.

And so, in my memory of that moment, is everything else. The beech trees have stopped swaying in the warm breeze; the bell birds have stopped issuing their distinctive chime.

I strip off my own pack and scurry down to where Chuck lies motionless.

The things Andy and I do for fun, most guys wouldn't do without the threat of a court-martial.

It's not that we like to torture ourselves by spending endless hours scrambling over rocks and hacking our way through thick forests. But we do love to fish and hunt in beautiful, pristine surroundings—and if that's the kind of experience you're after, you've either got to fly in to those unspoiled spots, or ride in on horseback, or walk. We've done all three in our many years of exploring the wilderness together, and we've always had a ball no matter how we got there. And usually we get in there on our two feet. Hiking is just the best way to see scenery, make a minimal impact on the environment—and prove to yourself that modern living hasn't softened you up that much yet.

Even fishing, depending on what you're going for, isn't always restful. For instance, we were up in Alaska not too long ago, and in the last week I caught a halibut weighing 267 pounds. See, what you do, you drop the bait down with about ten ounces of lead on the line about 200 feet down in the water. When a big one takes it, there's no stopping 'em. He swallows it, and then he just plain takes off. And you have to sit there, you can't stop him. He runs the boat until he gets tired and stops. Then you can start working him. You get him partway up and he'll go back down again, and with 267 pounds on the pole and forty pound test monofilament, you gotta be careful. And you gotta work *hard*. It took me two hours to get that thing up, constantly pulling forty to fifty pounds just fighting the guy.

There were four of us in the boat and we had to fit the damn fish in the boat too. We subdued it with a club, put a big shark hook in the mouth, and kind of bent him up to where you could take two or three turns around his tail with the rope that's tied to the hook. Then you could drag the sonovabitch into the boat.

It's not that dangerous, but a 267 pounder's sure one helluva big fish. The funny thing is, the recovery rate off a halibut is only forty-six percent, or about 125 pounds of meat there. So you really have to go for the big ones, because the smaller ones aren't worth all that effort. What you do is you use salmon heads. Which means you have to catch big salmon in the first place, 'cause a smaller halibut can't get his mouth around a really big salmon head. Now, not everybody thinks that way, I know. But that's the reason why I always go for the bigger salmon, and the biggest halibut come in as a bonus. Furthermore, nothing gets wasted.

The other important thing about fishing is concentration. You can't sit there yacking just because there's three other guys in the boat. That's not the reason why you're there in the first place. Anytime you're hunting or fishing you have to kind of settle into yourself and put your mind on what it is you're *doing*. Experience helps, but any which way you absolutely have to *concentrate*. It's sort of like writing a book or driving your car. You know, driving looks easy, everybody thinks they can do it. But if you don't have your mind on what you're doing, it can kill you.

Come to that, whether you're driving or fishing or hunting or just plain hiking—whatever—conditions can make one helluva difference. I mean, sometimes you just ride along, everything swimming easy, no problem, and other times the weather hits you, or there's no game and you get shot in the foot instead—whatever, it just feels like a bitch all the way. Then, *coping* with the bitch has to be what makes the experience satisfying.

Part of the trip that Andy and I made to New Zealand to do some trout fishing was that way. And it was a typical Anderson-Yeager jaunt.

At first Keith Hawkins—a well-built, wiry guy in his early thirties who had risen to the rank of captain in the New Zealand Wildlife Service—didn't know what to make of Andy and me. I don't think he knew I was the guy who broke the sound barrier. And he was only vaguely aware of what we'd done in the War, which made him guess (he told me later) that Andy and I were "at least fifty." When he found out that I was a well-weathered sixty-four, and that Andy was a year older, he was clearly worried about us surviving. After all, he'd planned a six- to seven-day hike that would take us through dense bush country to the headwaters of the Ruakituri River in the isolated Urewera National Park on the North Island. And here we were, a couple of guys who had supposedly come "down under" to address a meeting of chief executive officers. For all Keith knew, we could have been a couple of gray-haired, wing-tipped desk jockeys.

I can't say for certain, but I'd bet he chose Jerry Cray—a big, strapping Green Bay Packer kind of a guy who served as his sidekick on our trout-fishing expedition—for one main reason: Keith thought we'd eventually need to be carried back to civilization.

And he was almost right, as it turned out.

But I'm getting ahead of myself.

Keith's fears about us were calmed considerably as soon as we met at the Moose Lodge—a new and extremely plush place that was developed by New Zealand and American interests—and began to discuss our equipment.

"Could I possibly see your boots?" he asked kind of hesitantly.

"Sure," I said. And when I whipped them out of my closet and put them on the floor between us, he let out a sigh and smiled.

My footwear spoke volumes, and to him it was all good news.

Judging a man by his boots is a trick that dates back to the Old West and probably beyond. But it's still as useful as ever. My boots told Keith of my experience in the outdoors for two reasons. The first was that they were plain and ordinary, not those $125 high-tech part-nylon, part-Japanese calfskin jobs some fast-talking salesman tries to sell you at some fancy shoe store. I think I paid $39 for mine out of the Sears catalog, where they were described as "work shoes"; they have rawhide laces and composition soles and probably have been on the market for the last thirty years.

But the second and more important thing about my boots was that they were nicely broken in. Sitting there on the carpet of my Moose Lodge room, they looked as laid back and relaxed about the trip as I was. That told Keith that either I'd done a lot of hiking already or that I was at least smart enough to clomp around the house in them for a few months until they were soft as an old baseball mitt.

"These babies have been to the top of Mount Whitney," I told Keith. "That's the tallest peak in the continental United States, 14,495 feet. Andy's have been there too. You don't have to worry about us. We know what one guy's blisters can do to a whole camping party."

"Ah, yes, mate," Keith said, "ain't that the truth. Well, I think we're gonna be all right."

What Keith didn't know was that even if my feet were a mass of hot spots, I'd just keep going, making sure that no one would know from the way I walked or talked that anything was wrong. I know because I'd done it before, with boots I hadn't had time to break in well enough. The thing is, it's a matter of disciplining yourself to accept a less-than-perfect situation—something that goes back into childhood and family attitudes, and that in my case was reinforced in my military training. It's like when we were flying in our P-51 Mustangs and had problems: you shut up about what's ailing you and just keep going so you don't jeopardize the morale of everyone within hearing distance.

I don't know if Keith could understand that, but it obviously didn't matter. You just never saw a guy so happy to see a couple of pair of beat-up old boots.

We started out the next day in rather cushy fashion. Keith brought around his Toyota Landcruiser—complete with his faithful dog, Kate—for a late start at about nine A.M.

Our first destination was Lake Waikaremoana, which is within the Urewera National Park. The wheels were very necessary, however, because it turned out to be a four-hour drive over a dirt and gravel road. The scenery was impressive—in fact, with its steep and sudden hills, dramatic ridges, and granite outcroppings, the area reminded me of my old stomping grounds in Lincoln County, West Virginia, although much more lush.

Soon after we arrived, Keith took us for a little practice hike. That let us get a better feel for the terrain, and meanwhile he was watching to see how we did. We noticed that the earth cover in the park actually looked a lot more like Hawaii and the Philippines than like the North American woods. We attempted some fishing from a boat that afternoon and evening, unsuccessfully, I might add. But that's fishing, wherever you are: sometimes they just don't bite.

The four of us had breakfast and got off to an early start the following day. The first leg of our journey into the bush was by a "track" (New Zealander for trail), but after a while the "track" ended and we were walking entirely without the benefit of an established path. Sometimes the ferns were knee-high, and you couldn't see where your feet were going; that led to a lot of stumbling on roots, sticks, and stones, even on the part of our guides. Some of the vegetation we were plowing through was completely new to me. What Keith called beeches, for example, were smaller than the beech trees back home. Then there were leatherwood trees, and hook grass, both aptly named. And most everything was very damp.

On the trail Andy and I noticed that our New Zealand companions carried a different kind of pack from the ones we were used to seeing in the States. Theirs sat relatively low on their backs—and now, as we tramped along without benefit of a beaten track, we could see how that kind of design gave them an advantage. The hanging vines and low branches didn't trouble our guides the way they did us, with our Sierra-style packs, which sat high above our shoulders and managed to get snagged every few feet

Chuck and Bud with the day's bag of quail

Chuck with Jimmy Doolittle

Chuck and Bud like to explore different parts of the world—
seen here in the New Zealand forest

New Zealand—a rainbow on the upper Ruakituri River

Poacher's hut in forest, where Chuck and Bud spent the night

Glennis with rehbuck—in Germany

Chuck with bear—in Canada

Honkers

Alaska: Chuck, salmon, Don

Guide and Chuck with prize halibut—267 pounds, for which a large salmon was used as bait

Chuck and Glennis in Hawaii, deer hunting

unless we continually bent down and twisted ourselves around. Even though I run about thirty minutes each day the year round, partly to stay in shape for this kind of wilderness trek, I knew I was going to be muscle-sore in places I didn't even know I had.

One kind of vine was especially troublesome. It would grab you with small hooks that stuck in your clothing and pack. And the more you struggled to free yourself, the more entangled you became. The New Zealanders, who have a sense of humor about such things, call this annoying fact of life on the North Island the "lawyer vine." The fact that all of this greenery came right down to the water's edge made casting and fishing fairly difficult, except in selected spots.

"Maybe we should shoot ourselves a couple of your wild pigeons for dinner," I suggested with a smile. After all, Keith and Jerry had packed rifles—and a couple of those big, bright-colored birds had fluttered temptingly over our heads as we started looking for a campsite.

"Actually, they make good eating," Keith said. "The Maori natives shoot them all year round for food. The only problem is, I'd have to give us all a citation if we took some now. They happen to be out of season."

"Oh. So what do we do for dinner?" I wondered.

"We'll have to settle for something not very special, I'm afraid, this being our first night and the good fishing spots still a couple of days away," Keith said. "I suppose it'll just be something like horsecock and foreskin on a four-by-four with a little white jerk."

"Oh."

Laying on those unexplained slang terms, I knew, was just another way of feeling me and Andy out, seeing what kind of guys we were. That kind of teasing always seems to go on in the outdoors when one bunch of guys brings one or more newcomers into their territory. Andy and I used to tell guys who were unfamiliar with the Kern River valley in the Sierras about all the rattlesnakes in that area, just to put them on edge. Then while they were fishing, I'd sneak up behind them and put my flyrod between their legs and shake it real hard. They'd think it was a hissing rattler and half the time they'd jump in, and we'd have something to laugh about that night around the bullshit fire.

Keith, I knew, was putting me through a similar rite of initiation. He knew damn well I had no idea what he was talking about—but I didn't want to give him the satisfaction of seeing me raise my eyebrows.

"Well," I said, keeping a straight face, "if I'd known, I wouldn't have had all that horsecock and foreskin for lunch."

Later I found out that I was making more sense than I'd thought. What all those colorful terms added up to was a baloney and cheese sandwich on white bread with mayonnaise.

Keith and Jerry not only had interesting names for their rations, they had a whole different approach from Andy and me to packing food for a trip such as this. When we climb up the High Sierras each summer, weight is something we always consider to be extremely critical. We take NutraSweet simply because it is much lighter than sugar, and we could never consider toting such bulky stuff as cold cuts, bread, and cheese. Dehydrated oatmeal and maybe small amounts of nuts, raisins, and sourballs— that was about all we ever packed in to supplement our staple of fresh golden trout, which we eat at least twice a day even if we're up in the mountains for a month.

Our New Zealand friends—in contrast to our precise

scientific approach—just piled on the food. We could hardly believe it when we saw them packing that "horsecock" and "foreskin," not to mention jars of jam—and fresh milk in a goddamn glass bottle for their tea!

Tea was an important part of their daily ritual, even out there in the bush. That first day Jerry had gone ahead to the camp early, and by the time the rest of us arrived, he'd made a fire (as best you can with their perennially damp wood) and had a big pot, or "billy," hanging over it from what he quite reasonably referred to as a billyhook. When the water finally boiled, he threw in a handful of loose tea leaves, let it simmer for a while, then declared, "Ah, mates, what a luv-a-lee brew we have here tonight."

I wondered what some of our old campfire buddies would say if they could see Andy and me now.

The second day of our New Zealand "tramp" was an uneventful one. We worked our way along a ridge, staying on the high terrain. We were headed toward the Te Kei stream, where we set up camp for the night. The next morning we got up early and took off downstream for Tui Flats, a place named for the colorful birds that sometimes fluttered just over our heads as we walked through the thick forest. It was a beautiful if still difficult walk (goddamn lawyer vines!) that took us past a stunning waterfall.

"You're probably the first Americans that have ever been back here," Keith told us. But it wasn't completely virgin territory. We had to look long and hard to find it, but there in the middle of nowhere was a camouflaged (and illegally constructed) hut.

We didn't see the low one-room structure until we were right on top of it: there were ferns growing out of the roof, and the siding was painted brown and green. Keith, who had been tipped off to its existence, said it was probably used by poachers, who came to that area for New Zealand possum. They were valued highly for their fur. From time to time we had seen these small animals scurrying across our path as we trudged along. They seemed to be a good deal more active than the American variety and looked more like cats than the possum I used to catch in West Virginia so that we could all eat.

"I'd like to nab a few of those poachers while we're back here in the name of the Forest Service," Keith said. "But in the meantime why don't we just borrow their quarters for the night."

It was a pretty cozy deal too. There were two bunks in one end of the small hut, and a fireplace in the other. The chimney was made of wood, which gave me pause until I saw it was lined inside with tin from old cans. We gathered some wood (all of it damp; we never did have a roaring fire the whole time we were there), then reassembled our break-apart, backpack-style fishing gear and set out to get some trout.

We were at an area where several small streams fed into the Te Kei River, which featured some inviting-looking pools. "I'm gonna use this New Zealand lure I bought in Tuai," said Andy, holding up a blue artificial minnow waggler.

"Go ahead," I said, "but I'm gonna start out with a good ol' Mepps spinner." Then we started spin casting, figuring that we'd slowly work our way upstream. On my very first cast a huge rainbow saw my lure and followed it a ways before finally darting off. "It's only a matter of time," I told Andy—unnecessarily as it turned out, because on his second cast he hooked a rainbow that probably weighed fifteen pounds. Andy worked him in carefully once, but the fish took his line and ran back out into the deep part of the river. So then he started to work that rainbow in again, tightening the drag this time because he'd felt some snags on the first go-round. I watched silently as he brought that prize fish in and in until the damn thing, no doubt trying to make another run to open water, swished his tail and snapped the line.

We were less than thrilled with that development, yet encouraged by the size of the fish we'd seen. However, we didn't get a damn bite the rest of that evening or even the next day. Keith, I think, took our bad luck the hardest. "I can't tell you how disappointed I am, mates," he kept saying. "Believe it or not, this is real trout-fishing country."

"Aw, don't worry," I kidded him as we slogged back to the hut in a huge downpour, "your weather makes up for everything."

It didn't stop raining until about ten the next morning, by which time we'd hiked to the point where the Whakaretu meets the Te Kui to form the Ruakituri River. While Keith and Jerry were fixing lunch, Andy and I again got out our fishing poles, put them together, and walked down to the area where the streams join: a pretty and productive spot. On my third or fourth cast I hooked an 8-¾-pound, 27-¼-inch rainbow trout: the first—and largest—fish caught on the trip.

I knew its measurements instantly because Keith did his official duty as a Wildlife Service officer, even though he was technically off duty. Along with checking out the license and gear of every fisherman he encountered (and citing them for any violations, such as using a double- or triple-barbed hook), he recorded, in his log book, the length and weight of every trout that anyone had taken. "Thank goodness for the system down here," Andy said, "or that fish you caught would have been a twenty-pounder by the time you got finished telling about it."

Later Andy caught two more rainbows in quick succession; they weighed 5.075 and 6.1 pounds respectively, according to Keith. We filleted them on the spot and packed them away. And as we did, Keith showed us something I'd certainly never seen before. "Watch this," he said as he placed the trout guts in the water under a fair-sized rock so the swift current wouldn't carry them right away. "It won't take long." And sure enough, within a minute or two a large eel—like nothing you'd ever see in a trout stream back home—savagely grabbed the guts and retreated with them into his deep-water lair.

The world we had entered seemed to get more exotic with each step. At night we'd heard an owl-like bird called the mau pau, but in daylight, as we walked, the air was sometimes filled with the tinkling sound of the bell bird. Of the birds we saw, perhaps the most distinctive was the New Zealand Rifleman, so named because their plumage resembles an old-fashioned military uniform. We also saw the Paradise duck (which is half duck and half goose) and a much rarer species of fowl called the Blue duck. As we hiked along—we in our Sears work shoes and the New Zealanders in their "gumbies"—rubber boots that had a small horseshoe on the heel for better traction—Keith's dog, Kate, would root those Blue ducks out of the brush and make them fly, and each time she did, Keith would count them and record the number in his log book. He and Jerry were sure we'd run into some red deer— that's why they'd packed their rifles—but as things turned out, we never did see one, and so we never did have any fresh meat.

You've got to stay flexible in the wilderness, always have an alternate plan, expect the unexpected. In case we'd forgotten it, that lesson of outdoor life was driven home all too dramatically on day six of our journey.

We began the morning right on schedule. Before we

started this trip, Jerry had taken us for a tour around the park. We went in two vehicles, and it was decided that we'd leave one of them—Jerry's jeep—at a sheep station located on the lower Ruakituri River. That way our backpack trip could be a one-way affair, with no back-tracking. As we got into the homestretch, however, it became clear that we weren't going to reach our transportation simply by following the river. There was just no place to walk along the gorge. Instead, we had to move away from the Ruakituri and up some steep slopes. Our plan was to spend the night near the Waitangi Falls; Keith said that from there it was a fairly easy walk down the river to where the jeep was parked.

And so we tramped off the beaten track. After about an hour or more of rough going, a dry ravine lay before us and the only way to get on the other side of it was to walk across a big old log that spanned the gap. I didn't like the looks of that piece of timber, the way it was mossy and wet, but when the others made it across, I figured it'd be no problem. Besides, I'd been balancing myself on this kind of natural log bridge since I was a kid going back and forth across the Mud River around home. But when I got exactly halfway across, the rotten bark and wet moss slipped out from under my feet, and I dropped like a stone.

Instinctively, I twisted myself around so as to break the fall with my pack. And I did land on my back, though I hesitate to say that anything "cushioned" the impact. For a moment I felt nothing; I may have been unconscious. Then, suddenly, I hurt all over. I heard Andy, Keith, and Jerry yelling, "Chuck" and "General" as they scampered down the side of the ravine.

Had I broken my back? As I lay there, I thought of all the things I had to do, all the filled-in spaces on my calendar. Now, if there was something seriously wrong, I might have to spend who knows how long doing nothing but convalescing. In speeches I'd often told people that the secret of a successful retirement was to always be booked up four years in advance. That line never fails to get a little laugh, but I mean it. Having commitments keeps you motivated, stimulated, sane.

Did this mean we'd have to cut short our trip? Now emotion swept over me and it was not disappointment or sadness. I was just plain damned mad as hell.

Bud Anderson

We knew Chuck was alive when we heard this wicked stream of cuss words come up from the gorge. I breathed a sigh of relief, but then immediately thought, "What do we do now?" Internal injuries are very hard to diagnose, and if he needed emergency medical help out there in the bush, we were in serious trouble.

"When the general gets his breath back, we can ask how bad he's really hurting," Keith said to me after we'd gingerly slid Chuck out of his pack and helped him hobble over to a seat on a large boulder.

"Well, that's the truth," I said, "we can ask." Knowing Chuck the way I do, though, I knew that wouldn't yield much information.

And sure enough, a few minutes later Yeager was issuing his first statement: "I'm fine, no problem, okay." It's amazing to me, but more than ten years after his retirement from the Air Force, Chuck instinctively keeps up that fighter-pilot image, never showing stress or fatigue or pain, and always being upbeat about anything personal.

———————————

I was just happy nothing was broken. "I can walk fine," I told Andy. "Just help me get my pack on and we'll go." At first they all said "No way," but we debated it until they finally let me carry my own pack, but with some things taken out of it and distributed among the others. "Goddammit," I finally said, "the worst thing we can do is stand around arguing until I stiffen up."

It was just my luck that the bush was becoming truly junglelike at that point. But what could we do but press on? Gradually, we descended from the higher ground to the river. Sometimes there was a bank to walk on, but when it ran out on one side, we'd have to wade across through fast-moving water that was often almost waist-high.

I didn't say anything, but I was obviously not in the best shape for such tough going, and so Keith suggested that we make a change in our plans. Instead of all of us spending the last night of the trip at Waitangi Falls, he would cut ahead through the bush on his own, and reach the Toyota Landcruiser that afternoon. He'd then drive it to a spot Jerry knew that was about where we'd meet that evening and drive off to a back-country doctor's office so that I could get X rayed. I agreed, knowing that we could always go back out fishing someplace else the next day.

Before Keith left, though, a funny thing happened. We

spotted a camp inhabited by two fly fishermen—the first people we'd seen since we started our trip. Keith went down to check out their license and gear, and returned with the news that they were a couple of Americans—"From Davis, California," he said. "You know where that is?"

"Hell, yeah," I told him, "that's about fifty miles from Andy's house in Auburn, and seventy from my place in Grass Valley."

We made good time getting to the spot where Keith would meet us, and while we waited for him Jerry instinctively made a billy of tea. From there it was a one-and-a-half-hour drive to the doctor, who took some X rays, checked them out, and announced that I had a pinched vertebra, a stretched sternum, and assorted deep bruises. "You'll be okay," he said, "just very sore for a while." Considering the way I was hobbling around his office, that wasn't exactly a bold diagnosis. On the other hand, owing to the New Zealand system of socialized medicine it was, at least, free.

Keith and Jerry drove us back to the hut at Lake Waikaremoana, where we engaged in an impromptu exchange of gifts. I gave them our Teflon skillet, which we'd brought along and which had impressed them greatly. In return I got a beat-up old woolen jacket called a "swanie," something all New Zealanders seem to favor for their tramps through the woods. Then we said our good-byes and Keith promised to write soon, which he did, asking us to describe our trip for a presentation he was putting together to make the point that "older people" could handle themselves well in the deep bush country. "Don't forget to state your ages," he added, because he really wanted to make the point to his superiors in order to help get the area we had tramped over declared a wilderness. He was successful in that attempt, and I hope we contributed at least something. Even though Andy and I don't think of ourselves as your typical older person ...

The next day Andy asked me how I felt and I said, "Like fishing." So we pressed on with the schedule. The local conservator of wildlife, David Stack, drove us in his station wagon to Lake Taupo and we took a speedboat to a wildlife hut on a remote shore at a place called Waihaha for a couple of days of fishing. For about an hour and a half the waves hit that boat—slam, slap, slam—and at first I felt every jolt in my aching body. After a while, though, I figured out a way to stand in the boat with my knees relaxed a bit so that they became a kind of shock absorber for my body, like springs in a car.

Pain is one of those things that comes down to mind over matter. I don't fight it; I accept it when it's inevitable, and then I turn my thoughts elsewhere. The secret is to relax in the pain, to realize that it's there and so you'd better live with it. I'd be the first to piss and moan and get all uptight and self-pitying about being in severe discomfort—if I thought it would do any good. But I've been there—I've hurt bad—and I know that the only thing you can do when you're suffering is to keep going.

6

ON HUNTING

I am walking down a brush draw with steep canyon sides of rock and brush maybe a hundred feet high. I flush a covey of quail and they fly about one third of the way to the top of the canyon side. I follow and I can see them now and then scurrying to the top. Following them as fast as I can, I climb up the steep slope. I am winded as I approach the top.

The birds flush again, their wings whirring loudly. My shotgun seems to weigh twice as much as it should as I bring it up to my shoulder and squeeze off a shot. I watch one bird fall to earth, and as it does the others now fly to the next ridge. And so, after I pick up the downed bird, I go down the side of the canyon and up the other slope. And on and on until finally the birds scatter into singles.

I turn and see my best buddy, Andy, coming down a steep slope at top speed. Suddenly, he falls and there is a cloud of desert dust and a muffled sound. I rush over. He has split his gunstock, but there are no broken bones, thank goodness. In a few moments we both get our wind back and the quail hunt continues.

133

*   *   *

Quail hunting is probably the outdoor activity I enjoy doing the most. It satisfies my constant longing to be in natural, unspoiled places; it provides a physical and mental challenge—and because it's best when approached as a kind of team sport, it allows me to spend time with Bud Anderson.

Oh, and one more thing: it puts some damn good food on the table too.

I've always been drawn to a harder, more challenging kind of enjoyment, and quail hunting in particular really fills that bill.

Quail are one of the most challenging upland game birds to hunt, a real test of shooting skills and human reflexes. Hunting them is not a pastime for anyone who's out of shape or in the mood for a lazy afternoon's shoot. When you're out for quail, you must hunt on foot, and to be successful to any worthwhile degree you need to cover lots of open terrain and an equal amount of rocky and/or brambly places too. Quail is an elusive, fast-flying quarry, and pursuing them will give you about as much exercise as you want to get.

I didn't start hunting quail until relatively late in life: after Andy and I were stationed at Edwards Air Force Base in the early '60s, and we became somewhat obsessed with exploring the Mojave Desert and the nearby mountains. The reason I didn't pursue quail earlier in my hunting career was simple: the bird doesn't inhabit the hills of West Virginia.

One thing hunting teaches you, I guess, is patience. When I was a kid I knew the woods all around home. I knew the areas that were pretty well isolated, which places had the feed, where there were stands of beechnut trees, or hickory, or oaks for acorns. Usually what I'd do, I'd walk maybe two–three miles from the house to a good place where I knew there'd be squirrel. Then I'd set down and listen quietly. When it got to be just about beginning dawn they'd come out of their nests in hollow trees and start "cutting" on oaks. You could hear the cuttings fall on leaves and you'd set there waiting on early daylight so you could see the game. Then you'd sneak up on that squirrel and get within shooting distance with a .22, or a shotgun if you had one. That's the way I hunted then—rabbit, or squirrel or whatever. I didn't get to meet quail until a whole lot later.

Andy, on the other hand, grew up in quail country and has been pursuing these birds since his days as a farmboy near Newcastle, California. He and I, however, are of one mind when it comes to quail, and we both agree that there's just no comparison between what the scientific textbooks call *lophrtyx California vallicola* (or California valley quail) and other game birds. Glennis and I kept a quail called TDB (That Damn Bird) as a housepet for six years, and I know Andy feeds a covey of quail that comes around his backyard over in Auburn. Besides, we both have quail paintings and sketches as well as wood, ceramic, brass, and wax sculptures of quail all around our respective houses.

Why do we feel strongly about this particular bird? Well, dove and waterfowl such as ducks and geese give you excellent shooting, but basically the routine with those birds is that you have to just sit and wait for them to fly by. A real yawner, that can turn out to be. Chukar partridge and pheasant can provide both good exercise and challenging shooting, but in our opinion they are not as good eating as the quail, which is one of the tastiest upland game birds when prepared properly. Both Andy's and my family love the sight of real quail on the dinner table—which gives him and me a great excuse to hit the outdoors in search of those birds at a moment's notice as soon as the fall hunting season arrives.

Over the years we have settled on one area as our favorite spot, not only because of the abundance of quail there but because of its great natural beauty. It is down near the southern tip of the Sierra Nevada mountain range, on the eastern slopes. There in those foothills, where the desert joins the mountains, lies the Hansen Wilderness Ranch. I'd known Dr. Hansen since the middle '40s. On his land you will find water, feed, and cover—the basic necessities for quail propagation. And it's all private property, which makes it all the better, because that means that hunting is restricted to friends of the Hansen family, owners of the very large spread.

The ranch has a kind of unique beauty to it, combining, as it does, the severity of the desert and the relative lushness of the Sierra foothills. The high desert there is between 2000 and 3000 feet in elevation above sea level, and as you approach the ranch the terrain starts to rise and there is an intriguing network of hills, ridges, gullies, washes, and flats. There is even a peak of nearly 7000 feet and a heavy pine forest there, adding to the splendid variety. The lower foothills, where we do most of our hunting, are covered with shrubs and trees of varying density. Higher up there are oak trees, piñon, and digger pines, as well as manzanita shrubs. (Occasionally, we would drive up to the high elevations and harvest some piñon nuts, but you have to get there at just the right time or the squirrels will beat you to them.) The lower hills, draws, and flats are covered with grass, juniper, and creosote shrubs as well as a variety of sagebrush. In December, Andy and I always cut a few juniper limbs and bring them home for Christmas decorations.

It is, in other words, an endlessly fascinating area that puts the lie to the myth that the western states lack the interesting variety of vegetation you see back east. Here and there on the Hansens' place Andy and I find Mormon tea shrubs, which were used by Indians and pioneers for tea and medicinal purposes. In the lowest regions there are yucca shrubs and Joshua trees as well as several varieties of cactus and occasionally some Russian thistle, or tumbleweed—all common to the desert. The soil is sandy and rocky in those parts, and there are springs that provide clear, cold water the year round. The water forms creeks that get surrounded with willows and other shrubs. The creeks run down gullies and washes until they reach flat ground, at which point the water disappears into the coarse, sandy soil. In spots where the soil is slightly better, watercress thrives. Often, Andy and I harvest some to add to our lunch sandwiches or to bring home for salads.

Animals also abound on the Hansen place. In addition to the normal run of desert creatures—lizards, snakes, and gophers—there are coyotes, sidewinders, bobcats, rabbits, and squirrels. We also see hawks, owls, and roadrunners along with the occasional eagle. We've even heard that small bear and mountain lion have been seen in the upper, more remote regions, though we ourselves have never spotted either.

Over the years our typical quail hunt has evolved into a near ritual that starts the night before we set out. What we do first is check on the vehicle (preferably something with four-wheel drive, since there are only a few decent roads on the ranch), and then take stock of our equipment—guns, ammunition, paper sacks, water jug, and game bag. We also prepare the next day's lunch—usually the old standby of sandwiches made of turkey bologna, cheese, peeled green chili, and mustard on whole wheat bread.

We also pack along some fruit and maybe a couple of cookies.

Early on the morning of the hunt we fix a big thermos jug of hot decaffeinated coffee. We wear our well-broken-in boots that we use on our backpacking trips, blue jeans, and long sleeve shirts. We also take jackets in case of really cold weather or rain, and a baseball-style cap to keep the sun off our heads. You can get truly dramatic shifts in weather where we quail hunt—rain, sleet, snow, hail, fog, wind, and cold: all four seasons seem to roll by sometimes in a single day. Usually, though, we hunt in our shirtsleeves because we work up a sweat very quickly and, like long-distance runners, we stay warm through continuous exertion.

We always plan to arrive at the ranch around daybreak. After stopping to open the gate at the entrance, we "suit up," putting on our game bag and getting our guns out of their traveling cases. (The gun a person might take on a quail hunt is strictly a matter of personal preference; while many hunters like a 12-gauge shotgun, I prefer a 20-gauge because it feels lighter later, when you start getting tired.) If we bump into a covey of quail en route to one of our favorite spots, the hunt starts right there. The Hansens have names for various spots on the ranch such as Airplane Flats, Lone Pine Canyon, and Maude Anne Springs. We've adopted those as useful points of reference, and added a few of our own, including Chukar Hill, the Garden Spot, Hell Hole, and so on.

When we reach one of our many favorite spots we start the hunt in earnest. Andy and I have hunted so much together that we get our plan going with very few words. "You go around the hill that way," I might say. "Meanwhile, I'll go this way and meet you on the back side." It's understood that if one of us hears the other shoot, he comes running immediately.

Our ability to communicate without words never ceases to amaze me, even though it's been going on since the days when we flew in the same fighter plane formations over Germany in World War II. We can go through dense brush always knowing somehow where the other is located. There have been times when we've been separated and totally out of sight of each other for thirty minutes or more, but we've always emerged from the brush together, and at exactly the right spot, at the same time.

Call it telepathic communication, or whatever you will— all I know is that two can hunt so much better than one when it comes to quail. The first objective, of course, is to find a covey of quail; we hunt fairly well separated from each other at that point. As we walk along, we listen for quail calling to each other and look for signs of fresh tracks and for loose feathers. Once a covey flushes from the brush, we join up and hunt more effectively as a team.

The covey flushes with a startling burst of noise from the birds' strong wings, and usually the quail fly away in a pretty dense pack. The secret is to be able to locate the birds after the initial flush, follow them, shooting at each opportunity and being able to keep locating the individual birds as the covey flushes again, scatters, and hides.

Many quail hunters prefer to use hunting dogs to locate the quail and recover downed birds. We have found over the years, however, that in the arid regions a dog will "lose its nose" and become unable to follow a quail scent because of dryness, sand, and dust.

I have another problem with dogs: they are just not as good at quail hunting as I am. The quail cover is fairly thin in most spots on the Hansen place, and dogs tend to run ahead of you in an overeager manner and flush the birds while the hunter is still well behind and out of range. I'd rather act as my own bird dog. I have hunted quail so much that I can *think* like the quarry by now—which is the key to success in any kind of hunting. I have a sense of where the quail will go after they are flushed, and that makes all the difference between a good hunter and a mediocre one.

A downed or wounded quail is very difficult to find when it drops into cover. The quail's beautiful colors blend with the grasses and shrubs in a way that makes them practically invisible. Now, a well-trained dog *is* useful when it comes to finding downed birds. But since, all things considered, we'd rather not hunt with dogs, Andy and I have developed a simple technique for finding downed birds that we take great pride in. I will generally shoot only one bird out of a flushed covey and mark its position for pickup while I watch the direction of the fleeing birds. Shoot one bird, pick one bird up—that's our method. And it works. Let me tell you, there is nothing more frustrating—or wasteful—than demonstrating the skill of shooting doubles or triples and then being able to locate only one bird or maybe not picking up any at all! I take as much pride in not losing any downed birds as I do in getting my bag limit.

Andy and I get our limit of birds and then join up at the appointed spot and walk a mile or so back to the truck. It's always a good feeling, walking together, a little tired from all the exercise, satisfied by the weight of the birds in your game bag, not having to say much to each other, just feeling the enjoyment of being outdoors.

A kind of euphoria sets in.

Bud Anderson

Chuck is the best shot I've ever known. I was always pretty good with a gun, but I've learned to perfect my technique by watching Chuck and listening to his friendly advice. I might be able to outshoot Chuck now on a rare occasion, but you can generally bet on Chuck getting the most birds.

It's a funny thing about Chuck: he is an excellent skeet or trap shooter and yet there are probably many people who could equal or beat him in those areas. But when it comes to the real thing of hunting in the field, Yeager has few, if any, equals. There are many reasons for this, but what's unique about Yeager is his calmness. Quail burst out of the brush suddenly with that loud whirring of their wings that can unnerve many a hunter, even if the guy's expecting it. Chuck's gun comes up and is shouldered in one smooth action as he selects one single bird. He tracks the bird, waiting until it reaches the proper range to take advantage of the shot pattern. As the gun passes the bird in flight he keeps the gun moving, squeezing the trigger as the proper lead is achieved. The result: one bird down and needing to be picked up.

Shooting at the right range not only takes advantage of the maximum shot pattern, but it also results in less shot damage to the birds. And that, of course, means better meat for the table.

Chuck's ability to always remain calm and relaxed extends to every phase of hunting. Sometimes, early in the season when birds are more plentiful, we would get our limit of ten birds by nine or nine-thirty in the morning.

But if we are a few birds short, we'll break for lunch and I'm always amazed at how Chuck can lie down anywhere and instantly take himself a thirty-minute nap. Sometimes I can doze off, sometimes not. But Yeager is always fresh and ready to go back into the field and fill out our limit.

I like to tell about the tricks and jokes I've played on people, but there have been times, though I hate to admit it, when my friends have briefly gotten the best of me. Once two buddies of mine, Mal McIllwain and "Speck" Childs, invited me to hunt for bobwhite quail with them near Abilene, Texas. We all stayed up too late the night before talking and drinking, and so the next morning I wasn't a hundred percent myself and they decided to pull a fast one on me.

As we walked through the fields searching for quail, they always made sure I was between them. I didn't realize it at the time, but they wanted to make sure that when a bird flushed, one of them would always have a shot at the same quail that I was going for. And that's how it went: every time I would shoot, Mal or Speck would also shoulder their guns. A bird would go down and Mal would say, "Nice shot, Speck," as he broke his gun and picked up an empty shell case. Or if it was on the other side, Speck would say, "You got that one, Mal." This went on for about an hour and I was beginning to wonder about myself because, the way I saw it, *I* had shot every one of those damn birds.

Finally, they couldn't keep a straight face anymore, and

they broke down and told me what they were up to. As it turned out, I *hadn't* missed a single quail, and so after some good-natured cussin' I was able to share in the laughs.

Bud Anderson

Not everything that happens when we're out hunting is fun. There was a time when Chuck and I and another guy were quail hunting out in Jawbone Canyon, near a place called Breadbutter Springs. We had split up for a while and were reconnoitering, when our friend comes running up with a story about seeing a Volkswagen parked in the bushes and a man lying on the ground next to it. "Let's get out of here," he says. "Let's not get involved." But Chuck and I wouldn't have any of that. We started off immediately and, way back in the willows, we found this man lying facedown, with his arm bent under him kind of strangely. He looked like he was dead, and we rolled him over to see if there was a knife in him.

Well, one eye was open, the other closed. The man's whole face was contorted in a manner that suggested that he'd had a stroke. He showed signs of frostbite too; he'd obviously been out there all night.

We were sure the guy was dead, until he finally groaned. Then we got him some water, and in a little while he became sort of semiconscious.

Believe it or not, that friend of ours made another pitch

for not getting involved. "Let's leave him here," this guy actually says. "If something happens, we'll all be responsible and it'll be a big legal mess."

Well, Chuck would never hear of anything like that. He just looked at that guy and said, "Go back to our truck and get some blankets."

He did, and Chuck and I slid the blankets under the poor guy and we carried him out and lifted him into the bed of the truck. Chuck suggested we check the guy's wallet for some ID, and when we did, we found a Louisiana driver's license, an Alaska heavy equipment operator's license—and twenty-one hundred dollars in new hundred-dollar bills.

We began to drive him toward Mojave, when we ran into a highway patrolman, who radioed ahead to the hospital and told us, "Follow me." Then we took off at ninety mph down the highway. Once we got the man checked into Antelope Valley Hospital, the patrolman counted out the cash, using us as witnesses, and turned the money over to the local sheriff.

Then Chuck simply proceeded on to his next adventure. That's the way he is. He doesn't dwell on things, he's a man of action. I called the hospital about a month later to check on the guy we'd rescued. I found out that he had originally gone into the intensive care ward, but had improved steadily and in fact had just been released.

I relayed that information to Chuck but it really didn't register. Chuck's not terribly interested in looking backward. His philosophy of life might be summed up as "Okay, now. What happens next?"

There's no doubt about it in my mind: hunting builds character. I guess one of the reasons I get such a bang out of it, so to speak, is because there's always the element of the unexpected. Like the time Don and I were out for elk.

In Colorado there's an elk season that's especially for muzzle-loading rifles—the black powder variety—and I apply every year and got a permit a couple of years ago. The season opened Saturday morning, and Don and I went out into the woods before daylight. What you do is you listen for a bull to bugle—he's trying to gather his herd of cows up for the breeding season and his bugling clues you to where he might be. But on this morning we didn't hear anything, so we worked our way around the rimrock, through aspen trees, and set up a small camp about 1000 feet up. We smoked around all day. Didn't hear a single bull, although we saw some cows. Finally in the evening we heard these bulls bugling down over the edge of some rimrock, in some little pockets of aspen about 1000 feet below us.

So the next morning before light I dropped down to this one pocket. The wind was coming from the east—you always want to work upwind because elk can smell you real, real easy. I was working through the aspens real slow, daylight now, and spotted some cow elk grazing. Then I heard the bull bugle right behind the cows. I moved along real easy and kind of lay down next to a log in some weeds where it was damp and wet, no noise. The cows were feeding right toward me; eventually they got within twenty feet, and still no bull in sight. I could only see about a hundred yards through the aspens. But I knew he was there because I could hear him in back of them. Finally, the cows went on by me. They didn't smell me because the wind was coming from their direction. I waited about fifteen minutes. No bull. So I got up and headed toward where I'd heard him the last time, going along real slow and watching, watching. Suddenly about twenty yards away this big five-point bull stood up right under a big black spruce—he just stood up and looked me right in the eye.

I eased up the old muzzle-loader and cocked it back and put the bead right under his chin, and pulled the trigger. The damn gun just popped. He stood there looking at me, couldn't figure out who I was. I cocked the gun again, pulled the spent cap off the nipple and threw it away, got another from my pocket and stuck it on, raised up, put the bead right under his chin. The gun went pop again. I was bringing the rifle down to reload, had it at about a forty-five-degree angle, when it went off, *boom!* and the black powder lets out a cloud of smoke twenty feet across with leaves and dirt flying all over the place. Scared the hell out of me. Scared the hell out of that elk too. He just reared up and jumped straight in the air and hit the ground running, headed back up around the side of the hill.

In the meantime I've got a charge of powder stored in a little tube and another bullet and more caps in my pocket. I haven't taken my eyes off him and I bellered at him and he actually stopped and looked back at me while I'm trying to get this powder poured into the rifle barrel without spilling it. I finally got it in and got the bullet started down and I'm tapping it in when he starts to run again. So I yelled some more and he stopped and watched me tapping away while I'm thinking to myself I can sure sympathize with those old-timers who used to have single-shot black powder muzzle-loaders with the Indians coming at you and you're trying to load the damn thing.

Meanwhile my elk had started to move off again around the hill while I finished getting the powder in and the bullet in and the cap on. Just as I raised up he stopped. His neck was right between some aspen, offhand he was about a hundred yards away, and I held just under his chin again and shot. Finally, the gun went off, *boom!* when I wanted it to and boy, he dropped where he stood.

Don was off in another pocket and couldn't have heard my shot because of the wind. So I went ahead and bled my elk, gutted him out, and left him lay while I went on to pick up Don's track where I knew he was going in and finally found him. We came on back, laid the elk on his back, caped him out, skinned and quartered him, and Don went on down to the summer cabin where they keep horses and rode back with two. We tied two quarters to each horse and led the animals out. Boy, that was really good meat too.

On the other hand, it doesn't always work out so well. I remember an incident, way back, that occurred just before I joined the service, and which at the time made me feel like my education in the outdoors was really complete.

I was coon hunting up around Richwood, West Virginia, with my dad and ol' One-Eyed Schaefer, a half-blind sheriff from those parts who we'd met one day while fishing at a place called Cranberry Creek. It was a cool, crisp moonlit night and the three of us were tramping around together in the woods. It was probably around one A.M. and about all we had to help us find our way was this old carbide lamp, and of course Schaefer's two dogs—a big male and a little jip, or female. As we moved along, everything was quiet except for the sound of those dogs running coon in the inky blackness up ahead.

A less experienced hunter might have thought it was kind of spooky out there, but for us it was business as usual, until all of a sudden those dogs drastically changed their tune—from a steady barking to the damnedest yelping and growling you ever heard. Then we heard a truly blood-curdling dog-scream, followed by silence.

Dad, Schaefer, and I looked at each other as if to say "What the hell?"—and the old sheriff drew his .38.

We didn't have to wait long to find out what was happening. The next thing we knew there was the sound of brush breaking and Schaefer's little jip yipping and coming closer, running back in our direction: yip, yip, bang, crash. And then—Jesus Christ! She runs into our circle of light, and right behind her is the biggest damn black bear any of us have ever seen.

I think all of us, the bear included, jumped about a foot off the ground. There was something almost comical about the way that bear came to a screeching halt and just kind of looked at us—in the same shocked way that we were looking at it. We humans were probably the most taken aback, though, because we just stood there while the bear had the composure to scoot off and hide behind a tree for a minute before eventually disappearing again into the dark woods.

We pulled ourselves together and tracked it, but all we found was the male dog, dead, of course. He'd been bitten right through the back.

Normally, a dog and a bear wouldn't be enemies, but looking around at what you might call the scene of the crime, I was able to see why they'd tangled—and considerably more.

For one thing, that bear must have been eating beechnuts when the dog surprised her, because you could see all those little white things forming a symmetrical pattern around the wound. I also noticed, from checking the tracks around the spot, that the bear had been prowling around in those woods with a cub alongside her. That was a key point, because it told us why she had reacted so viciously. She was a mother protecting her own.

A country-boy's classic Friday night, that was. And I wouldn't trade it for anything. It gave me great satisfaction to know those kinds of things about nature and to know I could handle myself in the outdoors.

That's why I never felt self-conscious about my rural background or the way I talked when, in 1941, I enlisted and suddenly found myself thrown together with a lot of guys from all over the country. Many of them were college-educated, and some of them from places that were, believe it or not, slightly more sophisticated than Hamlin. But I was always proud of my rural background even if it did set me apart. I never felt it necessary to apologize or hesitate about anything because of my backwoods upbringing. As someone who could ride the tall pines for miles as a kid by climbing to the top, bending them down, and moving monkeylike from one to the other—and as a connoisseur of outdoor delicacies such as bear steaks, turtle legs, and stewed squirrel—I felt I'd be just fine, thank you, when it came to soldiering.

7

ON FRIENDSHIP

Hal Yeager

Chuck will never be confused with Leo Buscaglia. He is not the sort to hug and kiss and show emotion.

When I was growing up, his younger brother by ten years, I could only *sense* his concern; he never came right out and showed it.

Certainly, he spent a lot of time with me, teaching me how to hunt and fish, and how to make kites out of what we called horse weed, flour-and-water paste, and the paper they used to wrap your clothes in at the dry cleaner. But maybe the closest he ever came to an outward display of affection was when he passed down to me his collection of two or three thousand marbles. He'd won them shooting against kids in the neighborhood, and it was such a rare gesture, and I was so impressed by it, that I've kept those things to this day.

As a youngster Chuck mostly expressed his feelings—or maybe it's better to say distracted you from them—by

151

making a joke. Like I'd be standing around watching him
milk a cow and all of a sudden he'd twist the tit a little
and squirt a stream of warm milk into my face. It was in
that rough-and-tumble, sometimes downright obnoxious
way that he let you know you were accepted—that he
thought you were all right.

But then, none of us Yeagers expressed our feelings
directly; that's the way we were raised. I can remember
brimming with excitement when Chuck flew down from
Wright-Patterson Air Force Base in Dayton in a P-47 and
buzzed our little town of Hamlin early one morning before the War. Jeez, he came in just a few feet over the
rooftops. But then, I would never let the feeling boil over,
wouldn't go braggin' on him or anything like that, though
I was about to bust my buttons with pride.

It was the same when he pushed past Mach 1 in 1947. I
was about fifteen years old and delivering the Charleston
Gazette when the Air Force finally made the announce-
ment. I can recall seeing the stack of newspapers and the
headline on top that said, *Yeager Breaks Sound Barrier.*
Was I surprised? You bet. You see, Chuck has always
been a very disciplined individual and he hadn't breathed
a word about this to any of us in his family; it came as a
complete shock, especially since we assumed he'd already
hit his peak as a war hero. But as thrilled as I was, I
didn't forget myself to the point where I ran home and
told Mom and Dad. No, I just went ahead and finished
my paper route. One thing about us Yeagers is, when
we've got a job to do, we do carry it through to the end no
matter what, and we never let our emotions get in the
way. Which is not to say we don't let ourselves have
feelings.

No doubt about it: my best friend in the world is Bud Anderson. I respect Andy as a great fighter pilot, a world-class fisherman, and an all-around good guy. He knows how to handle himself in virtually any situation, and so I could always just relax and have fun with him, whether we were fishing for trout or flying a combat mission over Europe or Vietnam.

A lot of people who have palled around with us might be surprised to learn, though, that we weren't always such good friends. As a professional soldier in a shooting war I believed I couldn't permit myself the luxury of friendships. Let me tell you what I mean by that, and how my relationship with Andy evolved.

When we first met, during combat training in Tonopah, Nevada, Andy was a lieutenant and I was a flight officer, which is just a fancy name for an airplane mechanic. I was still naive about airplanes when I arrived at Tonopah in 1943, at age twenty. Consider that the first time I was ever in a P-39 I took it up to 10,000 or 20,000 feet above the desert—and thought there was something drastically wrong because with the throttle wide open, I was going only 220 miles per hour.

"What's the matter?" I asked my flight leader. "On the postcards they sell at the base it says the Airacobra is a 400-mph fighter." He had to suppress his smile and patiently explain that there was such a thing as true versus indicated airspeed. (*Indicated airspeed* is what the pilot sees on the instrument panel in the cockpit. *True airspeed* is the actual speed at which the aircraft is moving through the air. At high altitudes, where air density is much lighter than at sea level, the difference between *indicated* and *true* airspeed is great, the true airspeed being much higher. Naturally, aircraft manufacturers quote true airspeed when advertising their products.)

I had come into flight training as part of a soon-to-be-dismantled "flying sergeants" program that didn't require any college, and I felt slightly, well, *different* from a guy like Andy, who had had two years of junior college back in California. But the main reason we didn't pal around much at first was simply that even though we were in the same squadron—the 363rd—we were assigned to different flights. Our paths didn't cross much during the working day.

Still, it was flying that eventually began to draw us together. Now, I've been called one of the great pilots of my era, so I figure that at least gives me good cause to be a judge of other pilots. And I had never seen a guy fly a plane the way Andy could. I still haven't. He has a style that's so distinctive I can easily spot it from the ground. If I had to describe it in one word, it would be "crisp." There was nothing a bit sloppy about the way he maneuvered in the sky. And when it came to buzzing—a technically illegal maneuver we all indulged in like wild men—Anderson was simply the squadron's superstar. He'd swoop down the highway with the propeller of his P-39 about a foot off the ground, scaring the hell out of innocent motorists but impressing the rest of us recruits with his balls-out style.

That's the way all the truly successful guys trained for combat back in those days when the War was already raging in Europe and Japan and we were rarin' to be a part of it. Most of what we did went totally against the book, but our superiors, in their wisdom, tended to look the other way because they knew we were getting a true baptism by fire.

Our maneuvers were so realistic that a lot of our guys died in their P-39s before they ever got overseas. I myself experienced engine trouble one day and had to bail out and watch my Airacobra auger into the desert (one of three times I'd have to use the parachute in my career—and Andy was in the sky with me for all of them). That was my first real flirtation with disaster. I had the wind knocked out of me when the chute opened and don't remember landing. An old sheepherder found me unconscious, threw me across his pack horse, and brought me back to the base, where I spent the next many weeks recovering from injuries to my back.

Our approach to training in those days is still a subject of controversy because of the fatalities that resulted. But to my mind it was the right way to go. Those who survived were the cream of the crop—and Andy was what the French call the *crème de la crème*. I never told him this, but I tried to base my flying style on his. He was just so damn cool up there in training, and when he got into combat he wasn't a bit different. It didn't surprise me, after we were shipped to Europe, that he turned out to be the most successful pilot in our squadron, with a total of 17¼ kills (a quarter kill is when four guys can claim a hit on the same aircraft).

OTHER VOICES

Bud Anderson

You just never get bored hanging around with Chuck. I'm thinking now of this big military exercise that took place in Casper, Wyoming, just before we went overseas. That was a big B-24 base, and the bombers were involved as well as the fighter pilots. They had all these bomber formations up in the air, and they wanted us to "attack" them for the training experience.

Well, we went out there, charging through the bomber formations and making mock attacks. I remember pulling up off one pass, and I looked back and there was a P-39 underneath me, just smoking like crazy. I said to myself, boy, this is *realistic*, it actually looks like someone got shot down. Then damn if the door doesn't come off and . . . poof . . . out comes a guy with a parachute.

Chuck Yeager.

Somehow or other his engine had caught fire; the thing just overheated and he had to leave it.

But by then I knew that Chuck wasn't just another face in the crowd.

I suppose the first time I heard about him, it was by reputation. Since I was a flight leader at Tonopah, I discussed the skills of our new pilots with other flight leaders. A couple of them commented on this new hotshot, Chuck Yeager, a real promising recruit from the wilds of West Virginia.

The thing that struck me first about Chuck was not his flying ability but his distinctive voice and his damned cocky manner. He didn't apologize for the fact that he was really just a maintenance officer; we'd go out barhopping and he'd just take over—always had to be the leader. "We're going to *that* place," he'd say. Then if we'd try to make a move on a bunch of girls, Chuck would always be the one to decide who pursued whom. "I'll take that blond one, you take the brunette over there . . ." That sort of thing.

He was always pretty slick with the women, especially for a guy who frequently describes himself as "just a hillbilly." I can remember times when we'd fly to Pasa-

dena on the weekend, all duded up in our "dress pinks."
He'd ask a gal if he could help carry her groceries—and
wind up going home with her and spending the night!
Then he'd fly back the next day. "I always carry my
shaving kit; you never know when you're gonna get lucky,"
he'd say. He always had that incredible confidence.

But Andy was more than just a good pilot. When we did
wind up in the same honky-tonk joint on a couple of
occasions and got to talking, I could see he was a regular
guy with a kind of boyish enthusiasm about flying and a
rural background much like my own. His tales of growing
up on his family's fruit farm near Newcastle, California,
helping his dad pick those peaches, nectarines, and plums,
and spending his spare time shooting squirrels and fishing the local streams—they sounded a lot like my life in
Hamlin.

Andy also shared my interest in machinery. Not only
had he been driving his father's trucks and tractors since
he was about twelve, he told me, but he'd also learned
how to keep them running with a combination of baling
wire, duct tape, and old-fashioned country guile. I remember a story he liked to tell late at night, after we'd
had a few too many beers and he was feeling a little
sentimental. It was about the first time he was up in a
plane, at an early age. He was with his father, who had
bought them both a ride with one of those guys who
charged you a few dollars to fly you around for half an
hour. They were swooping down over their own farmhouse in an open-cockpit plane. It was a beautiful after-

noon and for a kid like Andy, who'd thought about nothing but flying since he could remember, the thrill was almost indescribable. "But you know what the best part about it was?" he'd say. "The smell of the hot engine oil wafting back at us."

As someone who could almost get misty-eyed about the water pumps and other machinery my father used in his natural-gas drilling business, I could really relate to that.

Not that Andy and I are carbon copies of each other by any means. For one thing, I was never fascinated with aviation as a kid. I hadn't even seen a plane on the ground until a Beechcraft was forced to land in a cornfield near Hamlin when I was in my early teens—and the sight of it sitting there didn't exactly stir anything deep within me.

But perhaps more significantly, Andy has always been very different from me in terms of temperament. He's the type who thinks long and hard about things and tends to see both sides of every story: I'm from the it's-either-black-or-white school, prone to make quick decisions and stick with them. Still, if I organized a little after-hours trip to shoot jackrabbits or quail in the hills near our training base, Anderson was always there, and we always had ourselves a good time and came back with enough fresh food to feed our whole unit. Our different temperaments never seemed to be a problem.

It wasn't hard to find places to hunt. I discovered early on that people are fascinated by fancy flying maneuvers. So I'd do the usual—fly over somebody's ranch, do a couple of rolls, then land my plane and go in and introduce myself. The stunt flying kind of broke the ice and, after we got to talking, most people were really friendly and more than willing to invite me back to hunt on their property.

Bud Anderson

Back when we were training for aerial combat in either Europe or the Far East—we had no idea where we were being shipped—Chuck and I managed to get in an awful lot of hunting and fishing. Though it was technically against regulations, he'd bum a jeep and a rifle and we'd go off into the boonies. We'd shoot rabbits, coyote, and—after we'd been transferred to Casper, Wyoming—antelope, which we'd bring back to the base so everybody could have a big feed. When we were first getting to know each other, we drove out into the fields near Oroville, California, in my 1939 Ford convertible to get some pheasants. We were sitting on the fender and I was holding my .22 pistol. "Let me have that a minute," Chuck said. I gave him the gun and . . . *pow* . . . he gets this rabbit that was a good fifty yards away. That impressed the hell out of me, and it also made me feel a little sense of kinship because I had superior vision too. Later on, when we'd be on actual combat missions together, Chuck and I would often be talking on the radio about things in the distance—things that some of the other guys had not even *seen* yet. As a fighter pilot, even today with all this modern, computerized weaponry, your greatest asset is your eyesight; I'm sure ours, on many occasions, saved our lives.

By the time we got shipped out to England, I had Andy pegged as a potential buddy, someone I might get to know better after the War, providing we both survived.

That's about as close as I let myself get to friendship in those days—because of the War. What I mean is, once we got overseas, we were in a situation where the guy you had breakfast with might be an empty chair at dinner. You had to cultivate an attitude of "So what?" about absolutely everybody. As cold as it sounds, you were basically a fighting machine for the duration of the War and that meant keeping every relationship on a level where if the other guy was suddenly gone—shot out of the sky—it wasn't as if you'd lost a friend. Otherwise, you'd start saying to yourself as you climbed in the cockpit each morning, "I wonder if they're gonna clobber me today like they clobbered old Joe." And once that happens, you're as good as gone, because sentiment and self-pity will just sap a fighter pilot's spirit and leave him unsure of himself. When guys are putting their ass on the line, someone like that shows up as a "weak sister." It's a condition marked by the frequent development of mysterious "engine trouble" that makes guys break out of formation and head back before encountering the enemy.

Andy, because he's in some ways a different kind of person from me, sometimes got closer to people than I ever would. He had a buddy from New Jersey named Eddie Simpson who got shot down over France and it shook him up pretty bad. He also had a friend from Loomis, California, which is near his hometown of Newcastle, a guy he'd known since they were kids. Jack Stacker and Andy were both crazy about aviation; they'd track airplanes going over their houses and then compare notes, and they read all the flying magazines. Jack married Ellie Cosby, a mutual friend from their high school days, and then got sent overseas a few months ahead of us—and was promptly shot down. Andy never said much about it, but I could see it affected him deeply—when he was on the ground.

In the air it was a different story entirely. While I was very much a fighter pilot no matter what the occasion, Andy was one of those aces with a split personality: a normal human being when away from the War but a terminally cocky, can-do type in combat, the last guy in the world to run from any kind of confrontation. When either of us had some kind of mechanical problem while escorting a box of bombers out over Germany, we'd just keep pressing on as long as we could—and we'd make sure we didn't mention it over the radio, so it wouldn't undermine the confidence of some of the less gung-ho guys.

Once actually in the War, no one had to tell me about keeping my distance from my fellow P-51 pilots. It took a lot of self-discipline, but I'd occasionally turn down invitations for a weekend of hell-raising in London by lying and saying, "No, thanks, I've got something to do."

In reality, I was dying to go off and explore the pleasures of blacked-out London town. My only alternative, moreover, was to bum around the base for two days by myself. But when I considered the pitfalls of being buddies with a bunch of guys who were being shot at by the Luftwaffe day after day, it was no contest. I'd rather be a loner.

Being a Yeager, I was naturally skilled at controlling my emotions anyway. Back home we just didn't believe in outward displays. Even when my older brother, Roy, at the age of six, accidentally shot and killed our little sister, Doris, Mom buried her feelings—so deeply that when Glennis asked her about the tragedy years later, she didn't want to talk about it, and never did. Dad didn't vent his grief over Doris's death either, at least not directly. Instead, he grabbed Roy and me soon after it happened and gave us some intensive lessons in how to handle firearms safely. I guess he felt he had to make something constructive out of the loss, which he did. Roy and I, and eventually our younger brother, Hal, Jr., retained his wise words on the subject of guns all of our lives. Unfortunately, Roy—a big, kind-hearted soul whom Glennis called "the gentle giant"—also kept his deep sorrow over the accident until he died of a heart attack at the age of forty.

The habit of self-control was so ingrained in me that I couldn't suddenly drop it when the War was over and become a gushing, slobbering sort of guy. I did let my hair down a bit on that last mission I flew with Andy, when we soared above Europe together in our Mustangs, revisiting the Pyrenees, the Alps, and other scenes of our wartime experience.

Certainly the War reinforced our family habit of reserve: maybe it's even a West Virginia habit, to kind of stand off and watch people at first as a way of sizing up who they are and where they're at. When you're an observer you're very much aware of all the ins and outs of a person, maybe even more than if you're involved. But you have to hold yourself back to do it.

For a while there, even after the War, I always stayed somewhat withdrawn, not just from Andy, but from Glennis and our four kids: Don, Mike, Sharon, and Susie. I'm not talking about anything major here; we went fishing and hiking in the Sierras and shared a lot of living and had a lot of fun together. But for a time, somewhere in my gut I maintained at least a little emotional distance, protecting myself in case anything ever happened to the people I cared about most.

Bud Anderson

It may sound hard to believe, considering the danger we faced on a daily basis flying missions over Germany and France, but I was disappointed when my tour of duty ended. I didn't want to stop flying and fighting. I didn't want to leave my buddies. And I certainly didn't want to be back in the States doing something safe and boring while there was still a war raging on the other side of the world.

So I volunteered for a second hitch.

Chuck understood the way I felt, I'm sure. After all, he fought hard for his right to continue flying his combat tour after he got shot down over France and escaped via the Pyrenees. But a lot of people, including my parents, thought I was just plain crazy for wanting to risk my life. The army wasn't so sure about a guy like me either; when someone volunteered for additional combat duty, the way I did, he was in for a session with a shrink. They wanted to be sure you understood you didn't have to fly more combat and that you had all your marbles. I guess I did all right, though, because my request was granted, and after flying seventy-four missions (300 hours) the first time around, and shooting down twelve and a quarter enemy planes plus another on the ground, I went back and flew forty-two additional missions (180 hours), scoring four additional kills in the air.

I did go home briefly, though, between my two tours of duty, and let me tell you, it was very strange, going from war-torn Europe to a quiet farm in northern California, especially when you knew you were headed back to the war. I didn't talk about my decision to go back much with my mom and dad, maybe because I felt a little guilty for doing something that would make them worry more, when they could have had a little relief at last. I just puttered around for about two weeks, feeling very out of place in my own hometown because the country needed me elsewhere, and then I hopped the train that would take me back to New York for another Atlantic crossing on an ocean liner.

I'm glad I went back, but I still have to say that the second tour was something of a disappointment. Some of my best friends, the guys I'd shared my first combat experiences with, were gone, finished with their tours or dead or missing in action. And the flying, while great, just wasn't quite the same when I knew what to expect. The best thing about that second hitch, I guess, was Chuck. He was there, he was a link to the old days when the guys who'd trained together at Tonopah arrived on the scene, and he was just plain fun to be with. The bond between us was forming.

Then suddenly, our fighting days were over for good. When we were asked to give our state of residence, so that the army would know where to ship us back to, I said I was from California. That allowed me to go visit Andy awhile (I spent my twenty-second birthday at his house, and his mom baked me a birthday cake). But the main reason I called myself a Californian was so that I could go pick up Glennis for our wedding trip back home to West Virginia.

With Andy and I both married, we had put in a request to be stationed together, but our orders posted us to Perrin Field in Texas, a part of the world neither of us knew very much about. On top of that, our assignment there sounded considerably less exciting than what we'd been doing in Europe. We'd be working as instructors with pilots—young guys who were on their way overseas to nail down a victory that was all but won at that point.

I wasn't looking forward to making the trip to Texas. It would be a long drive in Ellie and Andy's old Buick. And what was worse, we had to make it without Glennis, who had to go back to Oroville, California, to tie up some loose ends, collect her stuff, and come down on her own weeks later. There weren't any interstates in those days, and so we went through a lot of small towns on the way. The going was slow. And in practically every whistle stop along the way, we'd hit the local bar, drink Canadian Club and ginger ale, and eat hard-boiled eggs, which is what I was surviving on in those days to save money. If the bar had a jukebox, I'd spend a nickel to play "Sentimental Journey"—and sit there and think about Glennis.

We did have one bit of excitement on our way down to Texas. On about the second day out, Andy's car threw a rod and so I pulled a spark plug to relieve the pressure and we continued on into the little town of Carlsbad, New Mexico. The mechanic there said he didn't have the part, though, and that getting it would take a fair amount of time. "Well, what do we do now?" I said to Andy and Eleanor. They just shrugged their shoulders and we scuffled around, looking to kill time, until we finally saw this lake where there were rowboats for rent.

Eleanor wisely declined our invitation, but Andy and I went out on one and must have looked pretty hilarious, flailing around out there, going around in little circles, not really knowing what to do. We were laughing and hooting—but not for long, because all of a sudden there's this bunch of people bobbing around in the lake, and screaming for their lives. Apparently, the little metal rowboat they'd been in had gone down, just sunk, far from shore, and it looked like they couldn't swim.

Andy and I were obviously the only people around who could help. And we knew what we had to do instinctively. In a minute we had that boat of ours turned around in the right direction and we were pulling toward the folk threshing around in the water with the coordination of an Olympic crew team. It's interesting how an emergency always brings out the best in both of us.

We pulled four people out of the water and brought them into our boat. There were two others who we told to hang on to the side while we rowed for shore. Again, we pulled in perfect unison and had those people on dry land in a matter of minutes. Pretty soon the damn car was ready and we went on our way.

OTHER VOICES

Bud Anderson

One reason Yeager seems somehow larger than life to me is that wherever he goes and whatever he's doing, he seems to attract adventure. If you hang around with him long enough, you inevitably wind up watching the guy get himself out of a crisis in some airplane, or rescuing someone else in a life-threatening situation.

The story of how we hauled those people into our row-boat was anything but an isolated incident. I can recall a time when we were out in Arizona someplace, in the wee hours of the morning. We came around a bend in the highway and saw car parts scattered around and a pickup truck tilted over just off the shoulder of the road. The cab was completely turned on its side, and when we got close enough to stick our heads in, we could smell the booze wafting up out of there. We could also see, in the moon-light, that there was a young guy passed out at the wheel and a woman, kind of half conscious, lying next to him. What was really scary, though, was that we could hear but not see a crying baby.

It's funny how we never need to discuss what to do in those kinds of emergency situations. I just crawled up on the side of the cab, and Chuck grabbed me by my ankles and lowered me down. I found the baby right away, and when we got that little fella out he seemed to be basically okay. Next we got the woman out, and then the guy. He was still either too dazed or too drunk to talk, and he'd had one ear laid back pretty good, but he was going to be all right too. By that time the highway patrol had ar-rived, so Chuck and I left the situation in their hands and continued on down the highway.

―――――

When Andy and I finally made it to Perrin Field, in Texas, we began what was, depending on how you look at it, either one of the worst or best experiences of our young lives. The bad news was that the other officers in charge of pilot training hated us—and openly. And I can understand why: we'd been in combat—hell, we were real live *aces*—while they had never progressed beyond the classroom environment. They were guys who had settled into a kind of suburban home life and were probably feeling pretty edgy about it, what with the War still on and all. Meanwhile, there we were, a twenty-two-year-old captain (me) and a twenty-three-year-old major (Andy), wearing chestfuls of ribbons. We were the *real* Air Force.

I guess we flew that way, too, which made them all the madder. Our approach to instruction was, to hell with the textbook, this is the way it's *really* done. We'd get into such realistic dogfights out there over the Texas plains that a couple of times our students near to passed out from fright. Was that an unprofessional way to go about things? That's what some of those by-the-book officers said, of course. But I don't think so. The method Andy and I used tended to weed out the weak sisters pretty damn fast.

I've experienced professional jealousy practically since the first time I stepped into an airplane. Yet there's never been anything like the resentment Andy and I engendered out there in Perrin. We were ostracized, like lepers, and even the wives went out of their way to be bitchy to our wives. I've got a picture somewhere that's taken from the camp newspaper. It shows Andy and me, and the headline is something like *A Pair of Aces*, but you never saw two guys more miserable and sullen.

The good side of all this was that it brought Andy and me closer together. Since no one else would socialize with us, we had to hang around together or go visit each other in those awful, overpriced rented rooms we had because there was simply nothing else available. And secretly we got a kick out of all the other officers being jealous of us.

It made being an ace all the more enjoyable; we really felt like members of an elite fraternity.

Pretty soon Glennis and Ellie both got pregnant, and Andy and I had something else in common: morning-sick brides. Money was scarce and so for entertainment one day we took advantage of an obscure Army Air Corps rule that said officers could take their wives up in a plane once a year for thirty minutes. So we signed out two T-6s, which are single-engine prop trainers. Then we got our gals, flew around over Texas, and, as usual, made the best of a less-than-perfect situation.

I remember one time much later, after our friendship had grown over the years, and we were up in the Tehachapi Mountains in the early '60s, an incident occurred that so underscored our common traits and instincts it was almost eerie. Andy and I were hunting, or trying to, up in those mountains about sixty miles north of Edwards. It was a perfect southern California day, and the rugged scenery, to a couple of test pilots who spent too much time pushing themselves and their machines to the limit, was as tonic as ever. Our only problem, as the sun sank slowly behind the trees, was that we hadn't seen a damn deer all day.

The sensible thing would have been to turn around, tool the old Willys slowly back to our campsite before dark, cook up some soup and bacon—and then sit around the bullshit fire, retelling our old war stories. ("*Hey, remember when I hammered that guy over the Channel, and . . .*") But for some reason we just figured "What the hell," and pressed on even though it was very late afternoon.

Almost instantly, we were rewarded for our lack of good judgment. For here comes about 200 pounds of veni-

169

son, loping through the brush on a hill facing us from across a deep ravine.

"Andy, look," I say, but he already was.

That big buck's probably 300 yards away, and visible only intermittently at that. But Andy and I, with our unusually good eyesight, spot him simultaneously. And, without a word, I stop my old station wagon and we both slide out and raise our rifles.

For a moment it looks like we've lost him; the vegetation over there is thick enough to conceal an elephant. Then suddenly that big buck comes into a clearing about ten feet across. A shot rings out. He might have escaped, I think. But just as my gun kicked I thought I saw his back legs upend. I was about to say that much to Andy, when he asked me a strange question.

"Hey, did you fire?" he says.

"Hell, yes, I fired," I say. "Did you?"

We both smiled, realizing what had happened. We seemed to think so much alike in the outdoors, it was spooky. Or maybe it was that we both thought like the birds and animals we found ourselves pursuing.

In any case, what we'd just done was squeeze off a shot at exactly the same instant.

I hopped off the ridge and started making my way down the ravine, moving toward where the deer might be. Andy stayed behind to give me the often-used signals that would guide me specifically to the spot.

Then the signals stopped, and Andy began scooting down the hill to join me. That buck must be near, I thought. A few more steps up the hill, and there it was: a ten-pointer, killed clean.

We started dragging it out. It was getting dark quickly now, and we wanted to get back to the camp.

But then I noticed something on the carcass and I told Andy to stop for a second and look.

There were two bullet holes, about three inches apart, going right into the heart.

By the time we fought together in our second war—in Vietnam—Andy and I were beginning to realize that ours was a special friendship. Not that we had a particularly great time in Southeast Asia. That war was a festival of rules, a veritable celebration of often useless and senseless military regulations. I participated as a wing commander of the 405th Fighter Wing, based in the Philippines, but with units in Vietnam. You just can't compare that war to World War II, where combat was combat. Back then you went after the other guy, or, more precisely, if you were a pilot, the other guy's machine—and though you see a lot of bunk in old movies about fighter pilots having some "code" where they didn't shoot at each other in certain situations, or they flew by and dropped a glove over the spot where they shot somebody down—that's all a lot of romantic bull. We just opened fire and hoped we'd made a hit. And from where I sat in the cockpit of a P-51 Mustang, it seemed the Germans did the same.

But in Vietnam something was very different, and it wasn't the fighter pilots. Despite all you've heard and read about all the confused and hesitant young men we were supposed to have over there, the guys I commanded struck me as basically the same gung-ho, balls-out types that I'd flown with in Germany twenty years before. No, the truly new element was the political pressure coming our way from back home. Instead of being kind of carried off to war on a wave of patriotism as we were in the early '40s, instead of hearing about people planting victory gardens and putting lights in their windows, each morn-

171

ing's mail brought news of new restraints—and such incredibly detailed descriptions of what we could do to the enemy and when and where we could do it, we were soon packing along a rule book that looked like the Manhattan Yellow Pages.

But I'm not bitter about the experience; never was. I understand the two very simple truths about the Vietnam War. The first is we could have won it at any time. The second, winning would have brought us to the brink of a nuclear showdown with China—which even a hillbilly like me can see is not a good place to be. And so, as so often happens in life, our country was faced with making the best of an imperfect situation.

On a personal level, my two-year hitch as a wing commander during the Vietnam War was pretty much the same thing. Although I'd probably never say this from a podium for fear of being misunderstood or bent out of shape by the media, my bottom-line reaction to the whole thing was—and is—"Man, what a lousy war." But I'd never wallow in that kind of negative feeling. For me, the next step after finding myself in a less than totally wonderful situation is automatically, "Well, how can I enjoy myself while I'm here?"

As a full colonel in my mid-forties, I made the best of things partly by exploiting the accessibility I had to airplanes to go hunting with Andy all over the Far East. But mostly I enjoyed myself by plunging headlong into the war, such as it was. When you are a professional fighter pilot, the way I was, dogfighting is your destiny. You are always being pulled toward it. You know in your heart it's what you do best, and so you go out and do it for your country and you come back feeling at peace with yourself and fulfilled. It's as simple as that: if you're a mason by trade, you like to put up good walls, and that gives you a kind of pleasure beyond monetary payment, because not everybody could be doing what you're doing and with everything coming out so strong and straight. I'm just the same, only in a different trade. What Chuck Yeager *does* is fly and fight. Everything else is a pastime. I know that much about myself. And so I knew, back then, what I had to do to maintain my own mental serenity in that rule-ridden war: I went on 127 combat missions, including one with Andy—our first, we realized afterward, since that triumphant tour of the European skies twenty-two years earlier.

But I also did things that broadened my horizons a bit—things like going on a night patrol with my son Don, who was stationed near a place called Bong Son, with the army's 173rd Airborne Brigade. (Coincidentally, Andy, who was commanding a fighter wing of his own in Thailand, flew a mission with his son Jim at around the same time, dropping propaganda leaflets over the jungle.) I got a real kick out of seeing Don use his outdoor survival skills (some of which I'd taught him on camping trips in the Sierras) to effectively wage guerrilla warfare against the Viet Cong. And that earthy experience of crawling through the brush was an education to a career Air Force guy such as myself.

Of course, if Andy and I hadn't been career Air Force men, we never would have been able to reach all those far-flung locations we've been to over the years we've known each other. As professional fliers we had a life-style that in some ways was even better than that of the rich and famous people we sometimes saw traipsing around those exotic locales in their Abercrombie & Fitch gear. Whenever Andy and I grew slightly weary of whatever corner of the globe we happened to find ourselves in, usually all we had to do was sign out anything from a P-80 to a T-6 and fly off in almost any direction we wanted. The world was really our oyster for many years, and it was all perfectly legit. The Air Force didn't mind these "proficiency flights"; in fact, they encouraged them as a way of keeping both their planes and their pilots in top shape. Besides, our superiors were not about to bust the chops of two guys who almost never failed to come back with a large cache of such delicacies as quail and fresh-from-the-mountain-stream fish.

Andy and I have had so much fun over the years, it seemed only natural for him to help me out on my AC Delco television commercials. We actually did one straight —one that got on the air.

OTHER VOICES

Bud Anderson

Chuck was scheduled to do a commercial at the Northrop Hangar, right across the ramp from the McDonnell Hangar, where I worked at Edwards Air Force Base, and of course whenever Chuck was in town he stayed with us much of the time. Well, he calls and says, "Hey, I've got this PR gal from the AC Delco people, and the vice-president of the film company that's making the commercial. They want to meet you. Can I bring them over and then we'll all go out to dinner?" So they all came on over, and I'm chatting with this very attractive gal about the commercials Chuck's done, and I said, "Yeah, I'll bet he's already telling you how to do your commercials."

And she says without even batting an eye, "Oh, yes, sure. And he's usually right too."

Of course, what they were doing was to give him this fancy copy and he'd just tear it up and say, "Bull! I'll put it in my own words." So anyway, she invited me to go over the next day when they were shooting the commercial and have lunch and so on. So I did. And you know, what really astounded me, knowing Chuck, was his patience.

The whole bunch of them were right over in this hangar, where there are airplanes being worked on and Northrop people milling around. The production crew for the commercial had maybe a third of the hangar over in a corner. It's a really tremendous crew—a gal with a stopwatch and a clipboard with its detailed timing schedule, guys watching the monitors, electricians that can move things, others that can plug things in, the light people, the reflector people, the makeup people—the whole nine yards. They'd just started shooting. It had taken all morning just to get set up. . . . So Chuck gets over there by the airplane and he's supposed to walk over to a table and pick up a product and talk about it—filters, I think it was. He starts out—and it's "Cut!"—something's wrong. And he starts again and it's "Cut! General, you've got your head down." And again, "Cut! You overstepped the line there, Chuck," and "Oops, you've got to have the label toward the camera," and on and on. For twenty or more takes. And he's very patient, very positive, and it really impressed the hell out of me.

One time at Edwards they thought it would be good to get Andy into the act. So I give my usual spiel about not waiting for trouble to happen, and then I throw a spark plug up in the air. Andy is playing the part of a crew chief in a hangar where the F-20 is parked; he walks by and catches the spark plug and then gets in his car and starts it right up. Cut, print, no problem. But of course that wasn't good enough for Andy and me; we couldn't resist making some mischief.

"I want to do a take two," I told the director. And so we did another that was exactly the same as the real commercial, except that at the end I walk over to Andy with a spark plug and say, "Hey, buddy, which end of this thing goes in first?"

And Andy, who's all suited up to look like some kind of lab technician, he scratches his head and says, "Gee, Chuck, I think it's the threaded end."

That wasn't the first time I made a commercial that you'll never see on the air. I did a special "take two" on an AC Delco ad once for a group of executives and lawyers from General Motors, which owns AC Delco. They all came to this fancy dinner a couple of years ago expecting to see a sampling of the big new ad campaign. "Well," said the master of ceremonies for the evening, "here's what you got for your two million." Then the lights go out and the commercial comes on a big screen and there's me, decked out in my flight suit, and standing in an airplane hangar. Everything's fine until I open my mouth—and start to talk about Delco products in the most impenetrable West Virginia drawl I can muster. "I got this batt'ry har, and it's jes' chuck full o' pow'r" . . . stuff like that. In the audience there was a kind of stunned silence.

Then, before the bigwigs could recover from that first blow, we showed them another of our supposedly expensive efforts. In this one I'm back in the same airplane hangar and giving my standard pitch about the benefits of the company's batteries and spark plugs to an actor who's listening very intently. The guy is obviously impressed with what I'm saying about the Delco products, because when I'm finished he turns to the camera and says like he can hardly believe it, "No shit!"

Another silence. But that was quickly followed by a big laugh, after which we showed them the real commercials, which seemed to please them just fine.

If the commercials I've done have been good for the company—and I guess they have—it's because they've been so honest. My father always swore by General Motors products and he passed down that feeling to me. So what I say, I mean. And sometimes what I say, I wrote too. Not that I don't respect the fact that some high-paid writers have usually labored long and hard over the very small number of words in each spot, but I just can't bring myself to say something that rings false. Often it's only a slight change I'm talking about to make a line sound, you might say, more Yeagerish. I can recall one commercial where there was a shot of me driving a car around the Indianapolis Speedway, and the script called for me to say, "When I'm flying at low altitude, I need parts I can rely on," or something like that. I had them change the cue cards to simply, "When I'm flyin' real low . . ."

I don't mind working with cue cards, scripts, directors, cameramen, assistants, lights, cables, and all the other stuff that's part of the TV commercial business. That surprised the hell out of Andy when he first saw me endure the seemingly endless retakes. "Shoot, I didn't think you had the patience for the acting business," he said. But I told him what I'd realized early on—TV commercials are like anything else: if you're going to do it right, you can't rush it. The retakes are necessary because each little segment has to be not only well spoken, but of a precise length. It could get boring, I suppose, but I've learned to think of it as a challenge to kind of lock into a line-reading and be able to do it dead on, over and over, without sounding like a robot.

There's one thing I've learned about TV commercials: you don't know what fame is until you've been in one. Nothing I've ever done—in World War II, in my test-piloting years, in connection with *The Right Stuff*—has gotten me more notice and attention from the media as well as the general public. I don't mind signing autographs in restaurants or shaking hands with people in airports and hotel lobbies; in fact, most of the time I like to meet people that way. And that's a good thing, because the day those commercials came on the air my privacy went out the window.

8

THOSE FLYING MACHINES

Bud Anderson

A lot of people ask me what it's like to fly with Chuck Yeager. Well, probably no one is better qualified to answer that question than I am. I have known Chuck for some forty-six years. I was with him when he was really just learning to fly. I have flown combat missions with him over Europe in World War II—and twenty years later in Vietnam. I have been in the sky with him each of the three times when he's been forced to bail out. I have shared his flying career about as closely as any two pilots can over a long span.

And exactly what can I tell you as a result of all this observation? That if Yeager isn't the greatest pilot ever, he's certainly one of the greatest.

Flying with Chuck is a unique experience. By the time he has started the engine, taxied to the runway, taken

179

off, and made the first turn out of the traffic pattern, you know he's something special. His flying ability is way above average because he has a special love for machinery and an uncanny way of "feeling" himself as part of the airplane. In the air the airplane becomes an extension of himself. When he pushes the throttle to maximum he can "feel" the added stress and strain in his bones. It's something you can't really explain, something instinctive.

This ability applies to an "aerodynamic feel" of the airplane also. Chuck was a master at getting the most out of any aircraft he ever flew. In a tight turn he could bring it to a feathered edge, exacting maximum turn performance where a few more ounces of pull on the control stick meant the difference between smooth flight and a sudden loss of control—and sometimes between life and death in the air. It's like driving a car on ice and somehow instinctively knowing just how far you can go into a fast turn—then being able to back off and hold it just before it would skid.

I've seen people fly with Chuck who, because of his reputation, think that he's bound to start doing things that are wild and/or just plain dumb. But he doesn't because he loves to fly and wants others to enjoy it too. He flies smoothly and gently, not trying to impress anyone by taking them into the macho fighter-pilot world of high gravity forces, maximum rate of roll, or out-of-control gyrations. Being up there with him on a pleasure trip, you might even think, "How could a guy who flies so smoothly ever shoot down anyone in a dogfight?" Well, if some playful character was flying in the area and made a move on Chuck, you'd quickly see that he can do anything with an airplane that he has to do.

It wasn't just Chuck's flying ability, though, that made

him a great combat pilot. It was more an indivisible blend of qualities that made him so good. He had a unique awareness of the combat situation. He has that unusually fine eyesight. Plus, his aggressive nature served him well when it came to handling danger and emotional stress.

As a fighter pilot, Chuck had the rare ability to concentrate totally on the task at hand. In combat he could block out fatigue, fear, or any other distraction. His confidence grew with his successes, and this bolstered his already strong physical courage. Right from the beginning and without his knowing it, Chuck had the ideal profile of a leader. I mean, he was always calm, poised, and never flustered in the air. He never complained or griped when things were grim, setting the example for the rest of us, even those who outranked him. That optimism is ingrained in his nature, and you can see it even today. For Chuck, everything is always rosy, nothing is ever wrong or a problem. Accentuating the positive and moving on—that's his whole philosophy of life. And it's highly contagious. Another important aspect of his makeup helps him in flying; to Yeager, everything is right or wrong, yes or no. There is usually no gray area in between. So decision-making comes easily to Chuck. That may make him hard to live with sometimes, but it also permits him to make rapid assessments and decisions. That is, he'd weigh the odds, as anyone in a risk situation must, and decide immediately what the priorities were. He never took a chance where he didn't strongly believe he would come out all right. If he appeared reckless, it was a calculated, controlled, *knowledgeable* recklessness. Really knowing the odds when you are taking a chance— and then going ahead and taking the chance—is what research flying is all about. This ability served him especially well during his flight-testing days. Much of what he

Chuck smiles a thin, small smile—and a moment later, after some deft movements at the controls, we feel kind of a soft thud. Chuck had struck the bird squarely near the left wingtip, which minimized the danger to both airplane and occupants. The buzzard is plunging to earth somewhere west of Huntington—but we've got a dent in the leading edge of our wing about the size of a goddamn watermelon!

Now, to get that bird, on the first try like that . . . well, if you're a pilot, you know that would be an extremely difficult thing to do—far more difficult than that time, back around Tonopah, when he won the undying respect of his fellow recruits by sweeping down in his P-39 and purposely taking off the top of a tall tree. In any case, I remember sitting back there thinking—well, two things: first, how the hell was I going to explain that dent? The plane, you see, was signed out in my name. ("Aw, don't worry," Chuck said, probably reading the expression on my face, "we'll just report an accidental bird strike on the way home. . . .")

And second, the other thing that occurred to me—and not for the first time either—was hey, this sonovabitch can *fly!*

Call me a fighter pilot.

That sums me up pretty well, I think, because the term "fighter pilot" has to mean that you're aggressive enough to enjoy flying upside down and/or pulling heavy Gs—and gambler enough to take calculated risks and live to tell about it. Does that sound cocky? If so, it's no wonder, because I never met a fighter pilot who wasn't. Back in the War we used to live in drafty old Nissen huts and fly seven- or eight-hour missions every day in our P-51s, usually at altitudes of about 35,000 feet and without any kind of pressurization. To make matters worse, the British civil servants who ran the base insisted on closing down the mess hall at two each afternoon, just when the American fighter pilots were arriving back from their daily brush with death. As a result, all we had for lunch most days was a pathetic piece of bread with peanut butter and marmalade. I suppose we could have raised a stink and bitched about the conditions to anyone who'd listen. But we hardly seemed to notice; something else was fueling and comforting us back then, something that consumed our attention and energized us at the same time—which was to fight all day and then talk about fighting all night.

"Man," you'd say to your fellow P-51 pilots as you sat around bullshitting on your bunks each evening, "that sonovabitch came bearin' in on me and I outturned him and hammered him and he blew right up." Our conversations at night were almost as intense as the day's events, and at the same time provided us with a certain amount of laughs and release of the tension. There is no question that we were riding a continuous high that was goddamn exhilarating.

Part of that satisfaction came from doing something you're very good at. That's a feeling that anybody who's ever done anything really well can identify with. But then, if the particular skill you're using is relatively rare and you are practicing it with the relatively few who share and appreciate it, the whole feeling of functioning right up at the top of something goddamn wonderful gets emphasized. Not that we sat around analyzing it. We

Pakistan: Susie with
brown trout

Glennis and Chuck in Pakistan
in the early 1970s

Susie, Chuck, Sharon, Mickey, Glennis, and Don in Grass Valley in the early 1980s

Chuck and Glennis, Ellie and Bud—a double fortieth wedding anniversary

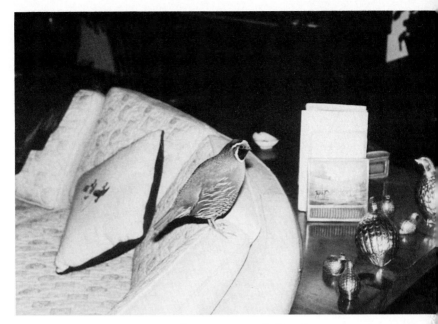

T.D.B. in living room with friends

Glennis and Chuck on deck of their home
(snapped by Chuck)

Pat (Susie's husband), grandson Cody supported by Glennis, Chuck, and Susie

Chuck, Joe Engle, and Bud at the Reno Air Races

Chuck in cockpit of P-51D, with Connie Bowlin and Ed Bowlin, who reconstructed *Glamorous Glen III*

The statue outside Hamlin
High School, in the town
where Chuck grew up

Bud sitting on wing of Mickey
Rupp's *Old Crow*—repeating
thumbs-up gesture from World
War II

Connie Bowlin and Chuck

Chuck and Bud doing AC Delco commercial with F-20
at Edwards Air Force Base

Glamorous Glen III and *Old Crow*
going straight up

were just doing an awful lot of what we did best. Living constantly with a calculated risk *and enjoying it* is a state of mind.

But it's a funny thing about this kind of mentality: while it's not common, neither is it confined to military men. I've seen fighter-pilot traits in all kinds of people: bold business people who make success happen by being honest and open to a clever gamble; men and women who keep living their own lives at full speed, without letting someone else's problems slow them down. A true fighter-pilot type is independent and proud of it.

He is not, in other words, like a bomber pilot. You find the bomber-pilot types in all walks of life, but in the military they are the people who fly the bigger, slower, less maneuverable planes, and who work best as part of a team. They might be able to do a more polished job of flying a heavy plane, but they have no interest in aerial acrobatics or what we call pushing the outside of the envelope. During the War their objective was to get there, no matter what the odds, and drop their bombs. It took guts and there's no question about that, but the mentality is absolutely not that of a fighter pilot.

Do I sound less than impartial about all this? In the Air Force there has always been a great rivalry between the two kinds of fliers, one that started during the War but lasted into the glory days of research flying in the late '40s and '50s. It didn't really matter what we were actually flying, if indeed we were flying anything at all. The fighter-pilot types didn't socialize with the bomber-pilot types; and when we were forced to work together, a lot of heavy-duty horseplay ensued, with us usually getting the best of it.

One way we'd find ourselves thrown together was when

three or four fighter pilots would have to go someplace to pick up some airplanes. The usual procedure was that we'd get hauled there in a C-47 Gooney Bird. Frequently, Bob Cardenas, who had flown the B-29 that had dropped me during the X-1 mission, got the job of chauffeuring me and my fighter-jock friends, and each time he knew he was in for some kind of trouble.

The Gooney Bird was a great plane to pull one of our favorite pranks. It didn't have seats—just a bench with lap belts where we passengers would sit—and beyond that the whole floor was open for hauling cargo. We knew that Cardenas was a good flier, very proud of his usually perfect landings. And so what we'd do was wait until he got the airplane set up and the landing gear down for his final approach. Then all of us fighter pilots would creep very slowly down to the back of the airplane. This moved the center of gravity, but since we made sure he had the flaps down first, Cardenas at this point wouldn't notice that anything was amiss.

We'd huddle in the tail together for a few moments, grinning at each other because we knew the best part was yet to come. Then, when Cardenas set himself up and trimmed the airplane up for a good landing, all of us would run like hell to the front. Now he's about fifty feet off the ground and the center of gravity has changed drastically. Invariably, the plane just heads down and *booms* against the runway a couple of times, making for one of the sorriest-looking—and funniest—landings you've ever seen.

Cardenas got back at us though. One time when we started our forward charge he just raised the gear and put on full power so that he pulled right back up into the air and then pushed over. This, as he well knew, created a zero-G situation. Suddenly, all of us smart-ass fighter pilots were pinned up against the Gooney Bird's ceiling. And there floating around with us are these toolboxes that must have weighed a hundred pounds along with these big gallon jugs of engine oil. It was damned dangerous, because he knew that at any minute he was going to pull back on the stick, and everything, us included, would just come crashing to the floor. But somehow the danger made it all the funnier, and we laughed just as hard when the joke was on us. We needed—all of us—to laugh.

OTHER VOICES

Bud Anderson

If there's one thing Chuck Yeager is, it's focused. He had the reputation of being independent and a rule bender— and so he is—but when it came to objectives, no one could be more single-minded. So you had the apparent contradiction of a highly individualized guy functioning very well in an organization known for its heavy rules and regulations—the military—because when the situation, the objectives, called for teamwork in squadron life, or in combat, Chuck was a team player. But when he got into the flight-test business, he was an individual. And that's very different. In flight tests you don't require teamwork; actually it's the other way around, you're very competitive. You want to be better than that other guy so you can get the next job or the next assignment. So that difference means that he was very much an individual, nonteam player. Yet in the total sense of getting the job done, no one knew better than Chuck that there's more than the pilot involved—it's the engineering, the maintenance, and the whole nine yards.

Now that my life is literally an open book, I get a lot of weird questions—well, weird to me anyway. Do I sleep well? Meaning, do I have nightmares about the more horrendous events of my life? Does my conscience bother me? Do I constantly rerun all kinds of scary movies in my mind; planes falling out of the sky over Europe and Vietnam; myself tumbling out of control in the X1-A; even the accidental shooting of my baby sister?

But the really constant theme with this kind of questioner is *combat*. Am I, they ask, "haunted" by the faces of the German guys that I shot out of the sky? And even, has it ever occurred to me that those pilots might now be bouncing their grandkids on their knees, or hiking around in the Alps just as I do each summer in the Sierras?

What these questioners seem to have forgotten is that the guys I shot down were trying to kill *me*. When people have screwed themselves up so thoroughly that they can't figure that basic fact of warfare—well, sarcasm seems downright cruel. Besides, I doubt it would reach them. So I just try to be straightforward: No, sorry, I just don't think that way. . . .

The fact is—and most of the people I meet as I travel the country seem to understand this intuitively—I sleep well. As an adult I've never dreamt about anything I can remember, except maybe golden trout and good-looking girls. When money was tight, and the bills were piling up, I figured, hell, I could just go out and shoot the family supper if I have to. And it didn't hurt knowing that in Glennis I had someone who knows how to butcher elk meat or make a squirrel stew. Self-sufficiency, for me, works better than Valium.

Another favorite question—have I ever been scared in combat? Well, no. You don't get scared in combat, there's too much going on, for one thing; and for another, you're real focused, and real high. You don't get scared because there's no time for any useless maneuver. If you can't do something about whatever is happening, if you have no control over the outcome—well, hell, you're wasting your time to worry about it. If you *can* do something, you're obviously totally involved in doing it. And that is really the answer, in combat flying or in test-piloting. If you're in a bad situation, it's what do you *do* first, and second, and third—and on down the line to get out of it. Still, I'll tell you, I was sure as hell scared that time in the NF-104 when I had to eject and my faceplate was smashed and burning. Fortunately, there's seldom time for anything but doing what you have to do next.

As for the tragic or frightening events that have happened in my life, they are just that—events that are part of the plot line that adds up to my life story. The close calls I've had as a test pilot? If I was forced to come up with a meaning for them, it would be this: I've had my share of good luck. The point is, I don't see things as punishments or rewards from Up Above, nor anything else outside the normal realm of reality. You know that old saying, "That's life"? Well, that's exactly what those—and all the other good and bad things that have happened to me—were: a natural part of living. It sounds cold sometimes when people say, "That's life," but you better believe it. What happens happens. Accept it and press on.

I survived the War, and even came away with a few good stories. I scored twelve and a half total kills, including five during one fine morning over occupied France. But the bottom line is, I got them before they got me, and there's no reason to give it another thought—except that people ask me about it, or want to hear me talk about those days in speeches. I do my best to make it interesting. The mental movies vary, although one thing always stays the same. Then and now. There are no faces in my combat memories, perhaps because I almost never saw them in the first place. Never even thought that way. What I saw were machines—big, beautiful machines. I fought the War from a mechanic's point of view. I never went into the sky thinking how many Germans I could kill, but how many of Hitler's machines could be destroyed.

I hope by pointing this out here that I can dispel another notion about me: that I valued combat as the *ultimate form of hunting*, the most dangerous *game*. Poetic bullshit. I may love to hunt, but being strapped into the cockpit of a fighter plane with your ass on the line bears little resemblance to tramping around, free and easy, in the great outdoors. In fact, there is absolutely no resemblance. Yet I guess you could say that the two great loves of my life are the outdoors and machines. Through my whole career I was able to take apart and put together every plane I ever flew, from the ground up. I'm not ashamed to admit that I have a *feel* for machines. I *know* when limits have been reached, I *know* when to back off—and it's not necessarily exactly the same each time in the same machine. This is not anything extrasensory. It comes from experience. People say a machine's just a machine. Well, I know that's not true. A machine has its moods, and if you're good with one, you'll know how it feels when something's getting ready to happen. You can't be afraid of it, but I've learned to respect the fact that the damn thing can start flying apart on you at a moment's notice.

Another question (a sensible one) is what's my favorite airplane? Well, there can be no doubt about that: it's the P-51—the Mustang I flew in World War II, the fighter pilot's ultimate airplane. Not only is the P-51 powerful and responsive, it's a beautiful plane to look at. And that's not all. The P-51 is the prettiest-*sounding* plane in the air, thanks to a big V-12 engine that purrs real low and deep. It's no wonder the airplane has attracted a huge following of buffs who read up on the P-51, collect pictures of it, and even rebuild their own with whatever parts they can get.

In 1987 there were about fifty P-51 Mustangs in flyable condition and more in various stages of restoration. Wartime Mustangs were built for about $60,000 in 1944. Later, P-51s were "surplused" and sold to the public for a few thousand dollars. These days a Mustang restored to mint condition could be valued at near $500,000. To own and fly a vintage warbird in the '80s takes a lot of drive, patience, skill, and money. Some are restored from complete wrecks or cannibalized from pieces of several planes. Others have been assembled from storage, flown, and passed on from owner to owner.

One of these classics, a P-51D, is owned and flown by Ed and Connie Bowlin of Griffin, Georgia. Both are professional airline pilots with Delta Airlines and they fly their impeccably maintained classic to airshows all over the U.S. They acquired the plane from Ritchie Rasmussen of Canada, who had rebuilt it from a near total wreck and flown it for several years. The Bowlins contacted me and asked if it was okay to paint their fighter plane like my wartime P-51D, *Glamorous Glen III*. I felt real good about that, met the Bowlins, and have flown their P-51D several times. It's really a thrill to fly that plane, and that's only the half of it: a pilot friend of theirs has painted *his* old Mustang to resemble Andy's *Old Crow*.

Bud Anderson

Mickey Rupp has owned five different P-51s. He's a friend of the Bowlins and they have often flown together to various events. Mick met Chuck with the Bowlins at Oshkosh, and over a few beers the suggestion came up that Mick repaint his latest Mustang into a replica of my *Old Crow*, the plane I flew in World War II. This way, Mick and the Bowlins could fly together as in the Ray Waddey painting "Double Trouble."

Mick went ahead with the idea—not an easy decision since his pride and joy had recently had a beautiful paint job. He checked with me for details, and one of the questions he asked me was where the name *Old Crow* came from. At first I told him what I always tell my Baptist acquaintances—that the fighter was named for the smartest bird in the air—but then I had to admit that my drinking friends know it was named after the famous Kentucky bourbon.

In fact, when I was training in the P-39s and was first able to have a "personal" aircraft, it always had a small *Old Crow* in plain white six-inch letters somewhere on the nose. I also had a small *Old Crow* on the nose under the exhaust stacks of our early P-51Bs, which were very plain, camouflaged with white noses and white stripes. After we were assigned bright colors for our group—red-and-yellow-checkered noses—and I had had a few victories, my crew and I decided, "Hell, let's paint the name *big*, up on the cowl, where you can really see it." Maybe I could attract more "customers" over the skies of Germany!

My wife, Ellie, likes to kid around about the name. She says, "Most men name their airplanes after their wives or sweethearts, like Chuck's *Glamorous Glennis*. What must everyone think I look like?" Of course I wasn't married, or even going with Ellie, when *Old Crow* was named. . . .

It was the Bowlins' *Glamorous Glen III* that I flew at the Reno Air Races in September 1987. Andy and I were both there, not to race, but so that I could give the winners of the big Pepsi contest a ride in the old Mustang.

Nick Jutte, Coldwater, Ohio

We were to fly in a P-51 Mustang, the same type of plane the General flew in World War II. I asked the General if he was going to do any rolls or loops and he said, "Don't worry about it!" When they put a parachute on me, I was nervous as hell.

We took off into the blue sky of Nevada and I relaxed a bit as we began to talk. I asked the General if there were any deer in the hills around Reno and he said, "Oh, hell, yes," and off we went to find some. We flew low over several ridges and the General said, "There go some, all females." But I couldn't even see them, let alone know what sex they were! So we made a turn and the General rolled the plane so I could see the deer. I was amazed at his eyesight. I asked him if he still enjoyed flying the P-51 and he said, "Oh, hell, yes! An airplane is an airplane, it's just like driving a car. . . ."

Tim Bowe, Stumptown, West Virginia

My flight with General Yeager in a rebuilt P-51 as a result of winning the Pepsi "Top Gun" Sweepstakes was an experience I will never forget. I had never flown in anything other than a commercial jet, so I was a little nervous, but I knew I was in good hands. Shortly after takeoff I told him that if he felt like doing a roll, I thought I could handle it. He told me to relax while he built up speed and then he did it. It was quite a thrill to look "up" and see the ground for a few seconds. I am deeply grateful to both General Yeager and Pepsi for making my first small plane ride such a memorable occasion.

In September 1987, the same month as the Reno Air Races, the Bowlins flew their Mustang to Nevada County Airport, near our home in Grass Valley, so that Glennis could see the beautiful replica of her namesake. Our two-year-old grandson Cody (Susie and Pat's boy) also came out to the airport to see and sit in Grandpa's airplane. We had a ball.

Man, flying in those P-51s sure brings back memories of the old days. That was before boosted controls, when you could actually feel the speed weighing on the ailerons, elevator, and rudder. The P-51 was—and is—a plane with character and class and confidence. It's the perfect plane for the true fighter pilot, who by definition needs to have those same qualities.

How did I—a guy who, as I've said, cultivated a reserved attitude toward other people—come to feel this strongly about something made of rubber and steel? The answer lies back among my earliest memories. It is a scene that probably happened many times though I see it in my mind as a single incident.

It is a West Virginia Sunday. My dad is home from work in the natural gas fields, and my big brother Roy and I are helping him service one of those single-cylinder water pumps that he used in his drilling. Now, the motors on those things are basically no different than the engines in my pickup truck or even the planes that I'd eventually fly; you had a piston that goes up and down in the cylinder and a gear that makes the spark plug ignite, and so on. But the beauty of Dad's pumps is that . . . all the elements are laid bare. The mysteries of the machine are revealed. And this allows Dad, in this long-ago memory, to explain to Roy and me how all the parts work together for a single purpose, according to a design and with no wasted effort.

There was the kind of vague enthusiasm in his voice as he spoke of those things that was not lost on Roy and me. It was something like hearing your father talk about his favorite ball team, an enthusiasm that was really shared. Roy and I, from that day on, were mesmerized by motors.

But there was more to it than that. It was through machines—which were part and parcel of our rural lifestyle—that Dad communicated love, or, more precisely, his trust, to us. He did this by letting Roy and me work on his pumps and, from a time before we were even teenagers, he also let us take care of his car.

There weren't too many bigger responsibilities in the Yeager household than that old Chevy. If the family car broke down, that meant a lot of money—money that we didn't always have. So we put in the gas for him, checked the water and oil, and hit all of the many lube points you had to keep greased in those days. We learned about engines and we also learned about seeing a job through to the end too. That in itself is a valuable lesson. Much later in life, at Edwards, I noticed that my ability to push through to the end of the task was a big difference between me and other test pilots. If the job was, say, to take the X1-A out to 2.5 Mach, and it started going haywire about 2.3, most other guys would back off and say, "Hey, I'm not here to get my ass busted." I had the discipline to keep going, to finish what I'd been told to do despite any distractions. Partly this was due to my combat experience, which is something most other test pilots didn't have. But the idea of finishing what I started was really ingrained in me much earlier, in the family garage. Roy and I were really young, and the job was relatively complicated. Still, we never intentionally missed a step. Roy and I would sooner have given up horehound candy, or our collection of marbles, or any of the other things we were devoted to, than disappoint Dad by missing a step in the car-servicing process.

That old car, in a way, was like a blank slate on which we said the things that, being Yeagers, we weren't about to say to each other outright. When Dad turned it over to us for servicing, the message was, "It's an important job, but I know you can handle it." When we gave it back, we were saying, "Thanks, we've done our best for you." It was communication. It was trust. It was respect. In any language, that adds up to a lot.

OTHER VOICES

Bud Anderson

My dad was a fruit farmer around Newcastle, California, and by the time I was twelve, I was driving his truck, loaded down with peaches, pears, plums, and nectarines, on the public roads. I was proud that I could shift the gears without grinding them. But the truck itself . . . well, we weren't the most prosperous farmers around and that Dodge was on its last legs. I remember going up a hill one time in Newcastle. The damn truck overheated, as usual, and stopped, and what I had to do, because the hand brake wouldn't hold, was to hop out with this big rock I carried and wedge it under one wheel to keep the truck from creeping backward down the hill. Twelve years old! And all by myself. What a thrill to have that kind of responsibility. I had to hold that thing together like that for four more years. When I was sixteen, Dad finally got a new truck, and because I'd done well, he turned it over to me. "You're in charge," I remember him saying. I'd change the oil and check the records faithfully. You don't forget a thing like that your entire life.

Chuck doesn't draw a distinction between automobiles and airplanes, and he's certainly right that the engines are basically the same. But for me aviation was always something separate and special. I developed a strong interest in airplanes at around the age of eight, and from reading magazines and listening to the Jimmy Allen program on the radio and by going to the movies, I got so that I could identify airplanes flying over our farmhouse by the sound. Me and my buddy, Jack Stacker, who lived five miles on down the airway, kept log books in which we'd jot down "P-12E heading west at 5:15 P.M." or some such, and later we'd compare notes. Chuck came into the service as a mechanic, but I knew I wanted to be a fighter pilot from around the age of twelve.

My dad, Clarence, Sr., had no special interest in aviation, but he catered to my enthusiasm as best he could. One thing we'd do from time to time was go to the

Oakland airport, just to see the planes. This was back around 1936–37, and they'd have the old Boeing 247s, DC-3 Gooney Birds, some navy airplanes, old amphibians. They held the National Air Races there one year, and for a kid like me, it was like going to the World Series. I took pictures with a little Brownie camera.

I guess I've passed down my reverence for engines to my sons, Don and Mickey, and even to my daughters, Susie and Sharon. They all know their way around a car, and I know that working on the family cars through the years has brought us closer together. The gospel of preventive maintenance that I preach in my TV commercials is something that came from my dad, and which I really have come to believe in. Heck, I even take apart the washing machine I bought Glennis back around 1968, change the drive belts, make sure the gears are lubricated. It may sound funny, the same guy who serves as a consultant on high-tech jet fighters, as I do, fooling around like that with a household appliance. But that washing machine is just as much a working system as, say, the F-4. And it would offend me to see it disrespected and just run into the ground. One way or another, it all hangs together.

What is the most fun sometimes is to find something in really sorry shape, and completely overhaul it. Not long ago my oldest son, Don, bought this beat-up 1973 Chevy pickup truck from the Forest Service in Colorado, where he has a ranch. He drove it awhile, and it was basically a good truck with heavy-duty suspension. But he needed something more reliable to haul his wife and kids around in.

"Bring it on out to Grass Valley," I told him, "and I'll make you a decent trade for it." He knew I was talking about my practically mint-condition '81 Chevy pickup.

Don was so excited about the deal he immediately made the 900-mile trip from his house to mine—through a heavy winter snowstorm. He used a full twenty-seven quarts of oil on the journey, or about a quart every thirty miles. I'll never forget the sight of him pulling into my driveway with thick black smoke oozing up from under his hood.

Man, if the AC Delco people had found out that the son of the guy who tells people "Don't wait for trouble to happen," was driving around in that disaster, they probably would have canceled my contract.

I was really delighted though. One man's wreck is another's reclamation project. And so as soon as I sent Don on his way back with my truck, I drove down to Dell Riebe's repair shop, pulled out the engine, and went to work. I got a new starter, distributor, generator, plugs, points, condenser, clutch, shocks, tires, window seals, floor mats—man, I was like a kid in a toy store. And it turned out beautifully. I use it for hauling wood and other chores, and I have a ball just driving it and keeping it maintained. Each time I get in the cab, I'm reminded of what was an unspectacular but truly satisfying experience.

Machines could never be mere hunks of metal to me. When I was preparing to drive the pace car at the Indianapolis 500 in 1986, I spent a lot of time in the racetrack's

Gasoline Alley, talking to the race drivers, and I heard that same sentiment expressed constantly. "Well," I remember A. J. Foyt saying, "I just knew I was on the verge of abusing my engine, so I backed down a bit." We were talking the same language of *knowing* seconds or even minutes before a problem develops that something is about to go wrong, and in both our cases we'd learned that language from years of hands-on experience.

There is just no substitute.

Nor is it just my opinion that mechanical ability is important to a flier. I've been told that a basic reason why I was chosen over the other test pilots to fly the X-1 was that I was the only one of the candidates who had a maintenance background; I knew what made that little plane fly. And one reason I was able to command respect as I rose through the ranks was that I spoke to the men and women under my command from practical experience instead of just parroting something I'd read in a textbook. You don't want everyone in the military to be like me, but it's nice to have at least one general with grease under his fingernails.

One more thought on this subject, and it's something I always passed along from my personal experience to the young test pilots at the school I ran at Edwards. The golden rule of safety is: know your egress systems. In other words, check out the available doors, windows, back-up systems, ejection seats, and other methods of escape as you enter a situation and *before* you reach a crisis point. I know, you may say to yourself, "But *I'll* never fly any research aircraft." Probably not. It doesn't matter. You are alive and living in the second half of the twentieth century. Therefore, at some point you will almost surely find yourself a) at a cocktail party, b) listening to a boring speech, c) watching a movie with no discernible story line but with a heavy message, and maybe even subtitles. That's when it really helps to know your egress systems so you can get the hell out of that situation as soon as possible.

Finally, the way I look at it, to have done what I did and survived, I must have been keenly aware of my own limitations as well as the limits of my machinery. And that, really, is what being safe is all about.

I don't own my own plane. Never have and probably never will. One reason is that I worked out a life-style where I get to fly pretty much what I want. I'm a consultant to Northrop, for whom I've flown such planes as the F-20, which is probably the most advanced fighter plane I've ever piloted. I also consult with the Air Force, an arrangement that brings me to Edwards about once a month to fly various aircraft and to discuss such topics as computerized weapon systems or cockpit design. Plus I do work with Piper, usually setting records from one point to another in order to generate publicity. So you can see that my flying options really run the gamut.

But the main reason I don't have my own plane sitting at the Grass Valley airport is that it just isn't practical. If I'm going to Los Angeles or San Francisco on business, it's just as easy for me—and just as much fun—to drive there in my Corvette. Why go through the hassle of driving to our local airport, flying to L.A., then renting a car and driving out of the airport to wherever I'm going? It just doesn't make sense. And as much as I love flying, I prefer to do things the simple and sensible way.

Bud Anderson

One more thing about Yeager that should be cleared up once and for all: Chuck says that luck and being in the right place at the right time had a lot to do with his many aviation accomplishments. Well, I don't completely go along with that. I'm always reminded of golfer Arnold Palmer's comment: "What a lucky shot—the harder I practice, the luckier I get. . . ." If a man has an opportunity, he has to recognize that fact, take advantage of it, and have the ability to follow through and do the job. Like many successful people, Chuck makes his own luck. He knows what to do when he gets the breaks. He's a tenacious son of a gun, and when he decides he wants to do something, it's going to get done.

That time he hit the buzzard demonstrates the several qualities that combine to make his handling of aircraft unique—superior eyesight, excellent coordination, a whole lot of flying, instant ability to calculate risk to man and machine, and, above all, his reaction to challenge. It does not matter, really, how important or how ridiculous the challenge—enemy aircraft or buzzard—he's there to take it on, and *enjoy* doing it.

If he is a little cocky about his abilities, that's okay with me. It's not bragging if you can back it up. And this guy has backed it up with all the spades in the deck.

9

WELCOME TO GRASS VALLEY

I live in a place where the soil is brick-red, the trees, mostly Ponderosa pines, are a deep, almost blue-green, and the women wear jeans, workshirts—and little gold nuggets around their necks. It's a solid kind of place, even if the earth underneath Grass Valley is honeycombed with hundreds of miles of abandoned mines.

This is the land of the gold rush, the place where the first traces of placer gold were panned, an area dotted with other hamlets named Rough and Ready, You Bet, Red Dog, and Humbug—which convey more of the local atmosphere. Grass Valley is in California, true, but this is not the California that people back east imagine when they hear the name mentioned. It's not surfing, fancy food, or anything else you associate with Los Angeles. Oh, sure, up the road apiece you'll find Nevada City, with its trendy pasta places and carefully restored Old West storefronts for the tourist trade. But the hottest restaurant in the town where I live is the kind of place you go to get over-easy eggs and hash browns from a pretty waitress in a pleasantly too-tight uniform.

If you're driving a Mercedes or Italian sports car over to Humpty's, a local spot, you'd best park it out back; otherwise you're bound to get some heavy stares as you come through the door. The people here tend to favor pickup trucks, jeeps, or other four-wheel-drive vehicles—and not because they're fashionable nowadays. No, if you live in Grass Valley, you've got to haul wood in the winter and, once or twice a year, make your way through deep snow. You need the right kind of equipment.

I remember the day Glennis and I moved here: April 1, 1975. We arrived late at night, so we spent the night in our trailer, which we'd parked just outside the garage. That was no problem, except that when we got up in the morning, I couldn't open the damned door—there was about two feet of heavy, wet snow piled up against it. Glennis just laughed and said, "Welcome to your California retirement home."

This is her country, and moving back here was for her a matter of coming full circle. Glennis was born in Grass Valley, in the old Jones Hospital, in 1924, and she grew up just a few miles north of here in Bangor. Her father farmed, mostly, but when times were tough he also worked as what they called a "powder monkey." That's the guy who sets the dynamite that was used for blasting through the hard rock of the mines. Her family has been in these parts for three generations and they were miners and farmers who knew how to work the land, from one direction or the other, with a plow or a pick-ax, in order to survive. Glennis herself learned early how to use a gun and a fishing rod, how to grow crops and butcher animals. So even though she's been all over the world since then, and has dined with presidents and princes, she has always been what you might call a real Grass Valley girl.

A strong, independent woman, in other words.

She bought the house we live in completely on her own. I had been transferred to Norton Air Force Base in San Bernardino, California, in 1973, to serve as the Air Force's Director of Safety—the last job I had in the military before I retired. Glennis was up in these parts one day to visit her mother and she happened to see this place. She made a good, firm offer and we wound up owning it. All I knew about it at the time was that it was a neat, twelve-year-old ranch house, with redwood siding, nestled on eight acres of typically rugged north California country-side. When I finally got around to seeing it with her some months later, I immediately liked the way it was set way off the road and up on a ridge, overlooking our pretty little lake.

"You did good," I told her. Then as we proceeded up the driveway, a bass broke the surface of the water, and I said, "No, honey, I take that back. You did just great."

Once we moved in we made a few changes that I guess reflect our personalities. We both hate an atmosphere that's dark, dreary, and depressing. Glennis's first move was to knock down several interior walls to open the place up so that you can sit in our big sunken living room and see up into the kitchen and her little office area as well as out the big picture window that overlooks the lake. The place now is light, bright, and airy. And with the hummingbirds, juncos, and towhees always hovering and hopping around the feeders on the deck, the distinction between what's outdoors and indoors is kind of nicely blurred.

For a long time, while we had TDB living with us, there was really no distinction at all between raw nature and civilization. TDB was a cock quail that I came upon probably just moments after he'd hatched. I was out on the property one day, putting in some fence posts, and I saw a hawk swoop down and grab this quail hen that I'm sure was TDB's mother. All that was left at the scene were some feathers and this pathetic-looking little chick. I knew if I left him there, the jaybirds would get him, so I scooped him up, carried him back to the house, and handed him over to Glennis.

She didn't think he'd make it through the night because he was all wet. But, knowing that a main worry in such situations is dehydration, she put some water down his throat and set him down next to one of those light bulbs with a wire cage over it. The next morning I took one look at him and said, "Well, he didn't make it." He was lying there with his neck just stretched out and hanging down. But then Glennis came over and made a "peep-peep" sound and he just jumped up and started hopping all around. I was amazed. But not Glennis. She just grabbed a pair of tweezers and dashed outside and in a few moments she was back with a cricket, which that thing gobbled down with gusto.

Within three or four days TDB was so strong in body and in mind that he just flat out refused to stay in his box. That's why we called him That Damn Bird; he would follow Glennis all around the house from dawn to dusk, keeping her company like no dog or cat ever could. Quail do covey in packs, so maybe he thought her feet were other quail. Or he had imprinted on her as Mom. But whatever the reason, TDB was never more than a few feet behind Glennis, and he'd hop right into her lap as soon as she sat down. Furthermore, he'd peck at the feet of any strangers who came in the house and got too close to her. In his opinion. He was an extremely opinionated bird, poking his beak into everything, getting underfoot when he couldn't get his beak in the way. There was good reason for his middle name. Glennis says it's a heck of a lot of trouble to raise a quail and absolutely does not recommend it to anybody. Just keeping after the droppings would try a saint's patience. Still, she spoiled that bird in a lot of ways, giving him orange juice every morning and an almond that she'd chewed up, mimicking the way a mother bird regurgitates food for its young. Every night TDB got some table scraps—spaghetti was his favorite, maybe because it looked like worms to him—and often a sip of white wine. He must have had a good head—I never saw him drunk.

He was a helluva lot more fun than your average pet and we enjoyed his company immensely. I guess we really liked him so much because this little thing you could hold in the palm of your hand was so damn self-confident and cocky. A real dominating personality. We took pictures of him talking on the telephone, looking through binoculars, and sitting up on Glennis's shoulder. Then one morning he just hopped up into her lap and died. It could have been a heart attack or a stroke or just old age. He'd been running the house more than six years. We buried TDB in our backyard, with little ceremony but much affection. Glennis and I, with our rural backgrounds, both understand that in the natural world things just come to an end, and that's the way it goes.

As for me, I don't keep pets, I keep vehicles. The garage is the only area that I've redecorated—and I do it with an ever-shifting array of cars, trucks, and RVs. I've also got several steel boxes full of tools, and there are tools in the trunk of each car and truck, tools on the shelves and windowsills and—hell, I've even had tools piled around the figurine on the Harmon Trophy, which I was privileged to win for my work in aviation in 1954, and which I like to keep in the place where I work.

Right now I've got a Chevy S-10 Blazer and Chevy 4x4 pickup truck, a Corvette, and a large motor home. If you're wondering how I fit all these into one garage, I don't. A couple of summers ago I went down to the local lumberyard and got myself some rough-sawed wood, and commenced putting up a second garage for the motor home. It was fun working by myself without any kind of plans or blueprints—West Virginia–style. And when I was finished, and shut the door and heard it click solidly, it was good knowing that I had built something with my bare hands that had turned out better than anything some professional contractor might have put up.

It also felt good knowing that the motor home wouldn't be just standing out there in the weather. When I need it, I want it to be ready to go. And the same goes for everything else I drive. I don't "collect" cars as a hobby. Every one of them has its individual uses. The motor home, for example, came in handy when I was taking Glennis on the four-hour drive down to Stanford Medical Center for her chemotherapy treatments. The 4x4 pickup I use for hauling wood and other supplies. The Corvette is what I use to make the one-hour-plus drive to the Sacramento airport when I'm heading out of town on a business trip. It's a beautifully designed car, and fun to drive, even the way I operate, which is to set the cruise control at a safe speed and just tool down the highway listening to a little country music on the radio and not worrying about a thing.

Even though my life has pivoted around the concept of speed, going fast in itself doesn't fascinate me. That's because my main purpose, in all of my research flying, was always to accomplish the particular goal we'd set for each project. If that involved squeezing all the speed we could out of an airplane, fine. Otherwise, what's the hurry? Besides, a lot of people would get a real chuckle at my expense if they read in the paper that I'd gotten a ticket for going forty-five in a thirty-mile-an-hour zone.

My little S-10 Blazer is the vehicle I use for simply getting around Grass Valley, or for hunting. This is the one I take on a more or less typical trip down to Dell Riebe's place. Dell, a good friend of mine, runs an auto-parts store that's not only the biggest in Nevada County, it's probably one of the most successful Napa dealerships in the whole country. At seventy or so, Dell's a gruff old guy, or at least he pretends to be, and having an early-morning cup of decaf with him, on those somewhat rare mornings when I find myself at home, has become something of a ritual.

Usually, I like to pick him up at his store. To me it's food for the soul, to start the day by seeing such a well-designed and beautifully run operation as Dell's. There's a beautiful smoothness to the way the parts come in from the wholesalers, get put on the stock shelves, catalogued in the computer, and then moved out to the customers who come in. There's something pleasing about the whole ebb and flow of things.

Then, after I kibitz with the stock clerks and kind of commune with bins full of gaskets, belts, and bearings, Riebe and I will head over to Hans' German Bakery for a donut and a cup of coffee. It's just a little place with a few iron-legged tables, but there's no reason Hans shouldn't prosper in Grass Valley the way Dell has. He's a real craftsman who learned how to bake in the old country, where they still teach people to have pride in their work.

211

I smile as I watch Dell checking out some toy Focke-Wulf fighter planes, obviously made in Germany, that Hans has hanging in little plastic bags near the cash register.

Dell is an old pilot himself, a barnstormer who used to sell rides in his biplane in the 1930s at rodeos in Montana and Wyoming. During the early part of the War he was a civilian flying instructor for the Army Air Corps. Later he entered military service in the army's Air Transport Command as an instrument instructor and ferry pilot, delivering many different kinds of aircraft around the country. But for all that, we hardly ever say a word to each other about airplanes. And sometimes we don't say anything much at all. Neither of us is given to small talk, to put it mildly, and we can spend long stretches just silently hanging out together. When we are moved to make a comment, it's usually something about how the town is changing, either for the better or worse.

Grass Valley is definitely a town in transition. On the one hand, you can see a continuing reliance on the rural values of understanding nature and tackling projects with common sense. When a new auto-repair place goes up in these parts, for example, you'll likely see the bays built facing east, so they can be warmed and illuminated by the morning sun. And right across the road from where I live there's a sawmill operation that is a study in old-fashioned efficiency and expertise. The logs come in during the summer and fall, and are piled under a sprinkler system. Ponderosa pines need to be kept wet, or else they will yield timber with blue streaks. Then the sawing goes on, all winter long. Finally, the wood is dried in big kilns and hauled away, and by that time the logs have started coming in again, and the whole process begins all over.

On the other hand, not everything that happens in Grass Valley is so pleasant to behold. The town is simply growing too fast. Just two miles from my house there's an intersection from which shopping malls spread in all directions as if no one had given a thought to planning, which probably they haven't. You can go out to buy a bunch of fishing lures or a new pair of hiking boots at certain times of the day—and hit the same sort of backed-up traffic you'd find in the suburbs of New York City. As we get more and more of the kind of people who commute to work in Sacramento, I'm also starting to detect the presence of big-city attitudes.

"Lawsuit" is a word that seems to have crept into the local vocabulary. I've never sued anyone, or been sued. And I'm steadfastly opposed to the idea of people, such as the families of the *Challenger* space shuttle disaster, being able to sue the United States government—and collect $750,000—in connection with the death of their loved ones. When any Air Force pilot augers in, his life is worth just as much. But his wife can't sue anybody, and that's proper because the guy took the job—and the risk—with his eyes wide open.

When I want to protect my rights I do so in the simplest and most direct way I can think of. For example, I wanted to firmly establish my property lines a few years ago, so I went around and personally pounded in the steel posts and stretched fencing wire between them. I enclosed all eight acres myself because I wanted the job done right and the land deed followed scrupulously. Then I put in good strong gates, and now there's nothing ambiguous about where my property begins.

Dell Riebe

It just goes to show you that you never know what to expect from life. If someone would have told me a few years ago that I'd become good friends with Chuck Yeager, I never would have believed them.

Yeager is a legendary name to me, so you can imagine my shock when I first saw him in my store, conversing with my salesman across the counter, one day back in 1975. That was nothing, though, compared to what was to come. The next time I walked in and saw Chuck he was *behind* the counter, waiting on customers like an employee. I guess someone had a question or a problem about a part, and Chuck hopped over there to help get things straightened out. I'm sure he knew what he was doing too. When it comes to having a love for, and an affinity with, the internal combustion engine, there's no one like Yeager. I'm sure that's why he survived so many close calls in the airplanes he flew. He knew what made them tick.

I've come to expect the unexpected from Chuck. He'll disappear for weeks at a time when he's off making speeches and test-piloting planes. Then, suddenly, I'll come in one day and he's helping my son, Bart, build an office on our upstairs level. Or he's filling orders for truck-bed hooks: a little side business I have downstairs. He's got energy to burn, and I guess that's why he's willing to work in my place for no pay. Of course, he originally came from a small backwoods town, so it's natural for him to fit in here. Not that we're backwoods exactly, but

214

there's not much glitter about Grass Valley. Then, too, his wife's from right around these parts, so I guess it must feel a lot like home.

By now I'm used to him dropping in whenever he feels like it, and it's other people who are shocked when they walk in off the street and see ... *goddammit, it's Chuck Yeager selling spark plugs behind the counter at Riebe's*! But if someone thinks it's weird for a famous guy to be working like that, well, Yeager figures that's their problem. The idea that he's reached a certain station in life and should act accordingly—that's just as foreign to him as Chinese. He just acts naturally and does what interests him. I suppose that's the way he's led his whole life.

———————————————————

Glennis is a farm girl and she conducts the business of Yeager, Inc., on an old pine table that we've hauled from household to household; if you look close, you can see the spots on it where, over the years, our four kids, now all grown and married, carved their initials in the soft wood while doing homework. Sitting there in her jeans and jogging shoes, Glennis positively exudes hominess—but don't let looks deceive you because, man, is she feisty on that telephone. I love to watch her field calls. We've never solicited a piece of business in our lives, but the offers still pour in and Glennis knows which ones I want to do (drive the pace car at the Indianapolis 500), which ones I ought to do gratis (a talk to the Air National Guard), and which ones to charge what used to be a good year's salary when I was what you might call officially working (an appearance before a group of cardiologists who are having a conference at an Alaskan fishing retreat).

I kid Glennis about coming from the take-it-or-leave-it school of negotiating. She was just as unbending with me, I remember, when I resisted her idea of setting up Yeager, Inc., back in 1980. Coming from a rural area of West Virginia, I've naturally got a kind of hillbilly mentality about certain things, and so I thought that not handling every phone call myself, and filing for corporation status, was kind of like putting on airs. "Hey, we've always kept things simple," I told Glennis. "Let's not change now." But soon I realized that, as usual in this kind of practical matter, she was right. I had to be as aggressive about handling fame as I am about flying.

I need Glennis's help because what I call the "hero business" has just never mattered much to me. Not that I'm a modest guy, but I hope I'm at least an honest one. And "hype" turns me off. I couldn't have cared less, for example, that the Air Force, for security reasons, didn't even announce that the X-1 had reached Mach 1 until 1948, nine months after we'd gone faster than the speed of sound. That was just fine with me. Ultimately, of course, the Air Force did call a press conference, and even though I still wasn't allowed to say much besides "Howdy," and "Yeah, I did it," I was on my way to becoming a sort of celebrity. Senators and congressmen from all over the country began demanding that I come to their district to address some civic group—and if a particular politician had clout in the area of military appropriations, the Air Force tried to comply.

I had to contend with some professional jealousy because the more places I went, the more famous I became and the more attention I got. I'm sure there are guys who resent me to this day for the way I always seemed to get singled out and put in the spotlight. That's their right, but I couldn't care less what they think. I never went around giving talks for the glory of it. Hell, those speeches were always *extra* work, and there were many times that I'd be flying solo back to Edwards from a talk and I'd be so tired I'd fall asleep at the controls, relying on a change in the drone of the engines to wake me so I could regain altitude, fly a bit, doze off, and there we'd go again. That was no fun, but I figured it was my duty as a member of the armed forces to go where I was sent and do what I was told. The only thing that really bothered me was when the guy who was supposed to introduce me at the Rotary Club luncheon or wherever was the obnoxious type who'd blow smoke in my face and ask me what I was famous for.

It was always harder for Glennis because even when I was at home I wasn't safe from the constant attention. I remember a film crew banging on our door in the middle of the night back around 1948, when we lived out in the desert, twenty-six miles from Edwards. Those guys barged into our little place and posed Glennis and me here and there and then demanded that we wake up our two little boys so they could shine those big lights in their eyes. Glennis did it, but all the time I could see she was as mad as a wet hen about the thoughtless way we were being treated—and in our own home to boot.

That night marked the beginning of Glennis's new, improved method of dealing with the media. What it comes down to is this: If we're gonna do anything, boys, it's gonna be on *my* terms. Even today we have a strict rule against videotaping anything or shooting still pictures inside the house. When the photographers persist, I just shrug and say, "Glennis's orders."

217

I've been to dinner at the White House a half-dozen times now, with four different presidents. The last time I was there they sat me next to Vice President George Bush. He's an old navy pilot, and so I guess we both felt we could talk straight.

"General Yeager, I've been dying to ask you," he said right off, "how do you get all that good press?"

"Well, sir," I said, "I've been doing it forty years now, so it's really no problem. All you've got to do is learn how to charm those reporters and, no matter what you say or do, you'll never get a negative story." We both had a good laugh over that because it's absolutely true.

ONE DAY IN MY LIFE

It was a typical morning in Grass Valley. Or so I thought—until I walked out of my bedroom at seven A.M. and saw the damnedest things scattered all over the living room.

Coming in late the night before, after a two-week tour of speaking engagements and TV commercial shoots, I hadn't noticed all this stuff. But now there it was: mountains of medals, trophies, and other mementos from World War II, my test-pilot years, Vietnam—virtually every stage of my career. The memorabilia was piled so high in some places you couldn't see out the big picture window that overlooks our hunk of north California countryside.

"Hey, honey, what's goin' on here?" I called to Glennis, who was out in the kitchen making us a cup of coffee. "Are we moving, or what?"

Of course I knew we really weren't. After thirty-five years of nomadic Air Force existence—of shuttling between Pakistan and Victorville, California; West Germany and West Virginia—we were settled into Grass Valley to stay. But, hell, I had to say *something*: our place suddenly looked like moving day at the goddamn Yeager museum.

It was kind of weird to see all that stuff all together at one time. Gingerly opening a box marked FILM, I could see Fox Movietone newsreel footage of Edwards Air Force Base in the '50s. Alongside it were 8mm home movies featuring, as I recalled, our four kids fooling around in various front yards or on fishing trips. And beneath those there were still photos of me in various stages of baldness. In another crate, called CORRESPONDENCE, I noticed, right on top, a laminated letter from President Ford advising me that I'd been awarded a special peacetime Congressional Medal of Honor. That was surely one of my proudest moments. But it was the funny-looking thing propped against the JayCees award for being one of the Outstanding Young Men of 1954 that really caught my eye. Probably to a non-flier it wouldn't look like much: just a ten-inch steel shaft, once silvery, but now, after forty years in various Yeager closets and attics, a kind of dull gray. It jumped out at me immediately as something special.

It was the pitot tube off the Bell X-1.

I picked it up and plopped down on the sofa. Normally, there's nothing terribly special about a pitot tube, which is an instrument that measures air pressure so that a pilot can find out how fast he's flying. But according to the plaque it came mounted on, this particular pitot tube had been on the nose of the X-1 on, as it said, "10-14-47." That's the day we reached Mach 1 . . . Muroc Air Base . . . the dawn of the space age. . . . That old plane part felt cool to the touch, but the memory it brought back was of a little orange aircraft sitting on Rogers Dry Lake bed and shimmering in the Mojave Desert heat . . . the *Glamorous Glennis,* I'd called the X-1.

The real Glennis, meanwhile, was just then coming into the room with two steaming coffee mugs—and a look on her face that said: Don't tell me you've forgotten what this is all about.

I didn't want to admit that I had. Research pilots—who get pretty vain about their ability to recall how their planes performed at every stage of each flight—would rather die before admitting they don't have perfect memories. So I figured I'd just tease her a bit and see if she'd tip her hand.

"You know," I said extravagantly, pretending to inspect that pitot tube from all angles, "if you're selling stuff off, this thing would probably fetch a pretty penny."

At least that drew a sarcastic little laugh out of her. Glennis realized I was joking—not that there wasn't truth in what I'd said about X-1 parts being worth something. After all, the rest of that plane is hanging in the Smithsonian Institution's Air and Space Museum in Washington, D.C., right next to Lindbergh's *Spirit of St. Louis.* It's an important part of aviation history. Still, Glennis knows I would never sell some old souvenir, or need to, the way she's managed our business affairs.

But like a schoolteacher who'd caught one of her students messing around in the supply cabinet, Glennis snatched the pitot tube out of my hand.

"You're not selling that thing to anybody," she said. "You're giving it away—to Marshall University." Then it all came back to me, of course. That school, which is located in Huntington, West Virginia, not far from where

I grew up, had announced that it was starting what it called the Yeager Scholars Program as a way of attracting the cream of the academic crop from high schools around the country. As part of the program, they'd asked if a collection of my memorabilia could be housed in their library.

Now, that was just fine with me because I'm not one to hang on to mementos. I guess it kind of goes against my nature to sit around and stare at a bunch of awards, or rest on my laurels in any way. Don't look back—that's been my motto ever since I was a kid—the kind of kid who was always wanting to see what was going to happen next.

Glennis understood my feelings (*and* the current tax laws regarding charitable donations), so she was also willing to give Marshall whatever they wanted. With one exception, that is: she wasn't going to part with our old love letters. I happened to watch her take the phone call when the school asked if our letters perhaps couldn't be sent along too. She was too diplomatic to say no outright, but I saw the look on her face and all I can say is, I wish Marshall a lot of luck.

I don't mean to give the impression that Glennis is some kind of sourpuss, turning down requests left and right. She can be downright sweet and motherly—I mean in the sense that she *responds*. One eighth-grade kid wrote in recently asking for samples from my trash can for a class project on "celebrity garbage." Glennis sent him a Coors beer cap—I drink a half bottle some nights—and a wrapper from a stick of Beeman's gum.

Then there are the letters that ask for advice in dealing with life's problems. My son is on drugs, some say. Or, I want to be a pilot but I can't make the grade for some reason. What should I do?

221

Glennis writes the responses and I sign them. Do whatever you can, they usually say, and then press on.

If the message is short, it's also sincere. When Glennis was diagnosed as having ovarian cancer in 1984, and had to undergo devastating chemotherapy that was in some ways worse than the disease, she'd be at that old pine table every day, answering the mail and the phone, pressing on. A year or so later, when doctors took 150 separate biopsies and told her that she'd licked that cancer against all odds, Glennis said that just sticking with her job and her daily routine gave her the mental serenity that allowed her body to fight back and win.

Now she's got cancer again. It came back in the spring of 1986, and this time I can see that the disease has sapped her spirit a bit and got her down. She keeps at her job, though, and tells me that even though it gets hectic sometimes, she's thankful for it.

OTHER VOICES

Glennis Yeager

When the doctors told me that I had actually beat cancer, back in 1985, they were more surprised than I was. I'll never forget how I heard about it. There I was, lying in bed at the Stanford University Medical Center, and this cheer goes up in the hallway. The doctor had just told the nurses that all 150 tissue samples they'd taken from various parts of my body had tested negative for cancer, and they were celebrating like it was New Year's Eve. He came in the room with a big smile on his face and said, "Well, every once in a while we win one, and this is one of those times."

Chuck was obviously pleased, too, of course, but all he had said to me during that first go-round was, "No problem, you'll beat it." He never let on how anxious he was: just let me see he took it for granted I would lick it. And, for me, that was probably the best thing he could have done.

Chuck's way to deal with emotional issues is often to appear not to deal with them at all. He simply refuses to go to funerals, even for some of his closest friends, and that's probably offended some people. He's got a gruff, bullish approach to death that can easily be construed as obnoxious. His big thing with me is to tease. "Well, when you're six feet under," he'll say. Or, "Don't you go kicking the bucket before you've got such and such done." I have counseled cancer patients, and if I ever used my husband's approach, I think the doctors would have me hauled away, probably to the psychiatric ward. But that's just Chuck's kind of convoluted way of thinking about the unthinkable.

My second diagnosis of cancer was just a real downer. I thought I had put my medical problems behind me for a while, and I just wasn't ready for any more. But I felt this lump down near my navel and after a few tests were run, I had to face the fact: I was a repeat victim of ovarian cancer. And if you check out the statistics, as I have in the course of doing some research on cancer, that is not a very good thing to be.

Ovarian cancer isn't confined to the ovaries; it can show up anywhere on your body, even on the tip of your nose. But what makes it really deadly is that there is no way to do a blood test, or any test, for it. You don't know it's there until you or the doctor can actually feel a tumor or see one with a CAT scan. By that time it's often too late to do anything about it.

My case is especially troublesome because, after they tried a second round of chemo, and I encountered complications with bone marrow dysfunction, the doctors decided my body just couldn't take that kind of all-out assault anymore.

For a while my immune system had been weakened so much that I got a bad infection in my knee, which spread to my feet and ankles and, before it subsided, left me with a bad case of arthritis. But the doctors have put me on a new experimental drug and I'm back on my exercise bike now. And I'm just glad I can keep busy with Yeager, Inc., business. I've got Cindy, our secretary, to help me now. Plus our daughter Susie. I trained her back in 1984 to take care of the books in case anything happened to me then, and now she takes care of all our business.

Chuck has made almost no adjustments in his globe-trotting life-style, and I think that's best.

My husband is a lot of things, but he's not a cure for cancer. And if he were hanging around the house all the time, it wouldn't make anything easier.

In fact, when I think of him constantly performing preventive maintenance on the washer and dryer, and looking over my shoulder as I do my paperwork, and giving me his suggestions on the best way to prepare gravy for the quail he's always just brought home from some hunting trip—honestly, I think it would make me just a little crazy to have him around one hundred percent of the time. Since he "retired," his time has been his own and his inclinations take him off to several different far corners. Through the years in service and in retirement I've become accustomed to paying him a lot of attention when he *is* home. On the other hand, I'm something of a press-on person, too, I've got plenty of work to get on with, and I need some time to myself to do it. Chuck understands that.

OTHER VOICES

Cindy Siegfried

I started working for the Yeagers in 1985, and from the first day, when the postman dropped off this huge pile of mail from book publishers and old friends, high-ranking executives and little kids, I knew it was going to be an interesting job. I think it was the Christmas card from President and Mrs. Ronald Reagan that really impressed me though. I mean, I know that the Yeagers have met several presidents, but being around them, and seeing how they live, you get to thinking of them as such regular people that when you're suddenly reminded of the General's status it comes as a kind of shock.

If someone sends a book to be autographed, or asks for a picture, the General does the signing personally. He won't tolerate one of those machines that reproduces your signature—and God knows he wouldn't let Glennis do it for him. It may take a while, and he may grumble a bit when he comes back from a trip and finds a huge stack of books waiting for him to sign, but they all get signed, repackaged, and sent back, often at the Yeagers' expense.

As far as answering the miscellaneous mail is concerned, the sometimes strange requests and the people who ask for advice on handling problems in their personal or family life, the Yeagers act as a team on those. Often Glennis will draft a response and the General will look it over and, occasionally, make a small change.

We get an awful lot of mail, though, that doesn't really require any response—just people writing in to say how much they admire the General. It's not really his war record that appeals to most people, I've discovered—or even his breaking the sound barrier. What most people admire is the way he's handled himself—how he hasn't changed.

———————————————

After thirty-four years in the military, I hate to be late, even if it's to see a friend for a cup of coffee. So I leave the memorabilia to Glennis, slap on one of my collection of 200-odd gimme caps, and head out the side door that leads to the garage.

"See you later," I call to her.

No kiss. It's not like I'm going to Europe.

The door slams behind me, and for a second I think of the screen doors slamming at Pancho's, out there in the high desert, where we partied so hard so many nights, including the nights before and after I went supersonic. Man, those were good times. But hell, if I'm reminiscing like this, I must have been in that goddamn Yeager museum too long.

Glennis looked like Vivien Leigh in those days.

Press on, press on, press on.

WELCOME TO GRASS VALLEY

*   *   *

Dell and I are sitting at a table down at Hans's place, which is close by the oldest Dodge dealership in the United States and across from a rather sad-looking antique store. We are staring out through the plate glass window into the fine cold rain. No, it may not sound like an all-expenses-paid trip to Las Vegas, but one thing you learn in life is that you don't have to go hell-raising to have fun, and so this is how we like to spend some time.

A few minutes before, Dell had been carrying on about how a sawmill had closed down and moved out of Nevada County under pressure from people who were worried about pollution. Now it was doing a booming business in another county. "We lost all them goddamn jobs," Dell said, "and now the prevailing southwesterlies blow all the smoke from their sawdust burnin' up over Grass Valley anyway." Man, he was madder than I've seen him since his wife, Skip, forced him to drive her to San Francisco one Sunday morning to look at furniture. Dell likes big cities even less than he likes what's happening to Grass Valley. But he calms down as suddenly as he erupts. And now no one was saying much of anything, and it was just fine.

Sitting there, I remembered another morning much like this, just after I got the news that Glennis had cancer for the first time.

"You know," I told Dell that day, "in the military we had a saying: If you can't move it, paint it. But for the first time in my life, I'm faced with something I can't do *anything* about. Can't move it, can't paint it."

Dell heard me out. And he said the only thing you could say to a guy in my situation. Absolutely nothing.

*   *   *

In a while I pushed back from the table and told Riebe I had to be getting home. "I've got to help Glennis pack some boxes of stuff we're sending to Marshall University," I said. "Tomorrow morning I'm heading out again, early."

"Where to this time, Chuck?" Dell asked.

"Oh, down to Marfa, Texas, to address the citizens—and get in a little quail hunting on the side. Then up to Alaska to give a talk to the people at Elmendorf Air Force Base—and get in a little salmon fishing on the side."

Riebe laughed. He knew I never cared much about the fee or the accommodations in these deals; I leave that stuff to Glennis. My one question, if the location was right, was "Can we squeeze in a little outdoor expedition?" Then the organizers can come fishing, hunting, or backpacking with me and we all get to know each other better. I've always found that you can size up people pretty quickly out in the woods, tell if they're city or country boys—or, more important, if they're the phony stuffed-shirt type or just regular guys.

The older I get, the more I realize how much I've relied on the outdoors all my life. As a kid I'd grab a .22 rifle and go hunting for squirrels in the hills around my house once the chores were done. And later, when I was training to be a pilot in those hectic early years of the War, I spent half my free time in the bars raising hell around Tonopah, Nevada, and other places—and the other half tramping around the hills hunting jackrabbits, deer, elk, and almost anything else that could be skinned or eaten.

Some of the other recruits probably thought I was crazy to be chasing wild game when I could have been pursuing wild women. The way I looked at it, there was time enough to do both—and there was at least one other young soldier who shared my opinion—and seemed to show up every time I tried to organize a hunting or fishing trip. His name is still Clarence Emil "Bud" Anderson—the best goddamn fighter pilot I ever saw. He lives just twenty miles south of Grass Valley, in Auburn, California. One reason I wanted to get an early start the next morning, in fact, was that I'd be stopping off to see him on the way to the Sacramento airport. We had some extremely important business to discuss—namely, which lures we should bring on our upcoming overseas fishing trip.

"Sounds like a pretty expensive junket," Riebe said when I told him the reason why I wanted to see Andy.

"Aw, you know me better than that, Dell," I said. "I'm not paying for any of this. I've worked a deal."

Dell shook his head and smiled.

"It pays to have a lot of friends," I said, "and to play all the angles."

"No doubt," Riebe said. "But come on back to the shop first. I've got some things for you."

I knew what he meant.

When we got back to the store, there were about two dozen copies of my autobiography, *Yeager,* sitting in a big box on Dell's desk, waiting to be autographed. I sat down and inscribed them all, then noticed a manila envelope full of pictures of the X-1 and the F-15, and scrawled my signature across those too. If I know it's for a pilot, I'll add, "Fly safe," or "I know you would have enjoyed flying this."

Around Grass Valley, people know that Riebe's Auto Parts is sort of a branch office for me. They can usually find Dell up in his office, a little wood-paneled room he's decorated with pictures of our planes. The local folks know they can leave something for me—a message, a book, or whatever—with him. And sometimes they might actually find me there, selling parts to the customers. Just like the people who get addicted to soap operas because of the characters, I'm a sucker for stories involving pistons, rods, and camshafts and their continuing relationships—and an auto parts store is the best place to hear them.

Even with Riebe's place serving as a kind of buffer, people will still occasionally make their way right up to our house, as off the beaten path as it is. We had a young kid who came all the way from West Germany once and pounded on the door and nearly scared Glennis out of her wits. I wasn't home, but she took the book he had with him and I signed it and sent it back. It could be we're not all that hard to find. Not long ago a kid cut a picture of me out of a magazine and glued it on the front of the envelope. He didn't put anything else, no address, no zip code, but his letter got delivered.

It's what's inside the envelopes that sometimes makes me scratch my head. When I left Riebe and got back to help pack the Marshall stuff that morning, I found that someone had sent me a fishing lure to autograph. (Not the easiest thing in the world to do, but okay.) Someone else wrote and said, "I know it's a long shot, but will you wear my size forty-six flight jacket around awhile and then send it back to me?" ("It's a long shot all right," I wrote back, "about four inches too long.") A few other people wanted to know if they could name various babies, streets, and racehorses after me. (Yes, of course, I would be honored, etc.)

And there was more. The people from Pepsi-Cola were thinking about having a contest in which the first prize would be a flight with me in a P-51 Mustang, at the Reno Air Races. A nice sum of money would be paid to me as a fee for my services; would I be interested? (Yes.) Could I address the National Congress of Aviation and Space Administration for free? (Sure.) A regular from our kook file just wants to let me know that he saw me walking around his backyard in Milwaukee. (Roger.) And a group of women aviators that I've put off once or twice before wants to know if I can talk to them anytime, anywhere.

That last kind of request is truly troublesome because I hate to turn people down—and yet I've got to draw the line somewhere. "Well, what do you want to do about them?" Glennis said, flipping open her appointment calendar. I took one look at all those filled-in boxes . . . an appearance at a big football bowl game in Phoenix . . . a talk before the McDonnell-Douglas management club in St. Louis . . . a trip to Korea for Northrop . . . a black-tie dinner for the Freedom Foundation at the Beverly Hilton . . . and I asked myself a very familiar question. Why the hell am I spending my retirement like this? Sometimes I feel like there's just too many balls in the air. I don't stay frustrated for long, though, because I know how to handle that feeling.

What I do mostly is chop wood. At the moment I've got more than a year's supply of good dry oak just waiting to be burned in the fireplace stove that heats our whole house. I get it from right here on the property, or maybe I'll haul in some big oak rounds from someplace nearby with the help of Pat, our daughter Susie's husband. Then, even though Pat's got a neat gasoline-powered woodsplitter, I'll chop it and stack it the old-fashioned way, with my sledgehammer and wedge, and put a little tin roof over it to keep it dry. If I'm not in a wood-chopping mood, I'll grab a pair of clippers and go clear out some of the blackberry bushes and brambles that always seem to need cutting back.

Working like that is good mental therapy and it's practical too. I recently climbed a 130-foot Ponderosa pine near the house to replace a coaxial television cable that the squirrels had eaten through. When I was finished I had not only cleared my head but we had better TV reception too.

You just never fail to get a feeling of accomplishment when you work on your own land. Every job has dignity—even digging a ditch in the ground to put in a length of pipe. I put in a whole underground system of pipes around our place, the idea being to carry water to drip-emitter valves that I installed by Glennis's favorite trees. Glennis loves nature the way some women love a fancy New York City department store. She might have a sugar pine over here that she's fond of, and over there she's planted an English laurel or blue spruce. Since it rains only between November and May in these parts, she naturally was worried about those trees surviving—until I installed the system that irrigates them at the rate of about four gallons an hour when the water is turned on.

I have to laugh at her sometimes, like when she planted a little redwood and asked me to put a drip-emitter valve on it.

"Jeez, honey," I said, "a redwood is one slow-growing tree. We're both gonna be long gone before that thing really takes root on its own."

I'm just as bad though. I have been stringing some electrical wiring down to a water pump and the other day I needed to put up a pole. I not only dug the hole much deeper than it really needed to be, I put a copper plate on the top of the pole just so it wouldn't get wet and rot out. Now, I guess, that post will last about four of my lifetimes instead of just two.

*　　*　　*

When I came back in to help with the Marshall memorabilia, the request to address those women fliers had either solved itself or, more likely, been solved by Glennis. In any case, it wasn't mentioned anymore that day, and if I heard about it again, it wouldn't be until I was headed out the door on another round of appearances.

Whenever I leave on these junkets, Glennis, as CEO of Yeager, Inc., always provides, not only a packet of airline tickets, but also a list of hotel names and phone numbers, rental car reservation numbers, and the names of the VIPs I should praise at the beginning of each speech.

As for my actual presentation, I never know what I'm going to say until I start to speak. It's been that way since the day I was first pushed to the front of a podium, back in the late '40s. I just can't bear to memorize anything, and if I read from notes I'm afraid it will come out sounding awfully unnatural. So I just try to say what's suitable—and give the audience a laugh or two.

Customizing a speech is just a matter of common sense. If I'm addressing a group at the Smithsonian's Air and Space Museum in Washington, for example, I figure there are a lot of aviation buffs in the crowd, and so my talks can get more than a little technical. If the audience is composed of middle-aged businessmen, though, I'm more apt to talk about my experiences shooting down German planes in my P-51 Mustang during World War II.

One story that both kinds of groups could relate to concerns the experimental G suits we fighter pilots were asked to try out in the middle of the War. Of course, the normal pull of gravity on the body, as we go about our daily business on the ground, is one G. But as you reached the maximum speed of 500 mph in a P-51, as you were going into a dive, say, to escape from a German attack, you might pull as much as six Gs, or enough to make the blood rush from your head and cause you to black out.

To prevent this, our scientists, in 1943, developed a flight suit with legs and torso that could be filled with water—the idea being that when you started to pull serious Gs, the water pressure would build, squeezing the legs and upper torso, and that would help keep the blood from leaving your brain. It worked pretty well—to a point. With these new suits we actually could lead the enemy into a steep dive knowing that he'd black out before we would, an advantage that would allow us to escape or maybe even swing around and shoot *him* out of the sky.

The problem was that once the legs of the G suit expanded, they stayed that way and we pilots would often have to spend the last three or four hours of the mission with these huge ice-cold water bags sloshing around our ankles. When we finally returned to the base in England, it was all we could do to waddle out on the wing and relieve ourselves after the long mission. While we were at it, we'd open the valve that was in each leg of the flight suit and relieve that too. From certain angles, it looked pretty strange to see a guy standing there with *three* streams of water coming out of him.

I call Glennis each night from the road when I'm on a speaking trip (always starting out with, "Hello, Mrs. Yeager") but she rarely if ever comes along. I don't think either of us has ever felt the need to be together constantly. Besides, Glennis hates to travel; she gets airsick and carsick and misses fielding the phone calls and handling the mail back home.

The Marshall project was just another example of her

managerial skill. The school wasn't simply scooping up a bunch of my souvenirs; it was starting a Society for Yeager Scholars, an ongoing project that she helped design. They had worked out a curriculum that allows the students selected for the Society to concentrate on what interests them, and not concern themselves with any of the extra fluff. I liked that, because it made education sound like more fun than I remembered it—and because it reflected the way I've lived my life.

You could look at what we were sending the university and see that I'm a pretty focused person. In other words, there were plenty of pictures and other things relating to the planes I personally had flown—and still do—but practically nothing about any other kinds of aircraft. Aviation history in general—the Wright brothers and all that—just doesn't concern me.

But when it comes to the space shuttle, I've always found that to be a much more interesting project from a pilot's standpoint. And the *Challenger* disaster of February 1986 hasn't changed my mind. Still, I wouldn't want to fly on it because to give a shuttle seat to someone like myself would be only a publicity stunt, which is something that at this point in the program NASA doesn't need any more of. Better to let a younger man get the experience, a guy with most of his flying ahead of him.

. . . A guy like the one whose apple-cheeked image was flickering on the living room wall.

That was me—in one of the old home movies Glennis had so carefully packed in the box for Marshall—and which I couldn't resist taking out and slapping onto the projector. Suddenly, there were all the Yeagers again. Or at least some of us: our two sons, Don and Mike, were crawling around in diapers in the front yard of our home

235

west of Rosamond, California; the girls, Sharon and Susie, hadn't been born yet.

In one scene I am pulling a trout out of some river. I look at the Western-style brass belt buckle I am wearing in that forty-year-old piece of film and notice that it's the same one I'm wearing now.

Then the film jumps; we're at a different house, on a different lawn, and Glennis walks through looking like Scarlett O'Hara.

"Aw, go on," she says when I tell her that. "What you're probably looking at is that old Ford of yours parked there in the background."

I had not noticed, but now that she mentioned it, I stopped the projector to get a better look. That was the first car we owned as a married couple—an old 1946 Ford. I fussed over it so much that I wound up redesigning the whole dashboard to make it more like an airplane cockpit. I put in an altimeter, fuel and oil pressure gauges, and, just for the hell of it, idiot lights, which only indicate, when on, that you have a problem, but not how *much* of a problem—that is, low fuel or no fuel—it's all the same to idiot lights, which is how they got their name. . . .

I started the projector again, and for a moment felt just a twinge of regret that we were giving these home movies away. Glennis must have seen the look in my eye. "Don't worry," she said, smiling, "I've already put them all on a videocassette."

Of course, even after these souvenirs were shipped off to Marshall, we'd still be surrounded by memories of our life together. Glennis had decorated the house in what she jokingly calls Air Force contemporary: there are paintings from Korea, a tapestry from Pakistan, pewter from West Germany—something from just about everywhere we've ever been. Aside from an appreciation for beautiful old wood, I myself don't have an eye for art. (My sole contribution to our interior decorating has been to ask her to move a portrait of a Gypsy mandolin player into the living room because to me the guy has bedroom eyes.) Glennis has made some very wise investments with paintings that she bought for a few hundred dollars in Europe years ago, and which are now worth several thousand.

That's how that particular day ended: with me watching old home movies and Glennis jumping up every once in a while to get the phone. As I was changing reels I heard her tell some New York City deal-maker type, "No, it's not that the money isn't sufficient. It's just that Chuck doesn't endorse products he doesn't use, and like, himself."

There was a pause while the guy absorbed that shocking news. Then Glennis added, "Believe me. I know him."

Ain't that the truth.

10

THE HAMLIN
HIGH SCHOOL
STATUE

Bud Anderson

In late September of 1987 I received a telephone call from
Joseph W. Hunnicutt, telling us about an affair to be held
in Huntington, West Virginia, on October 14, to honor
Chuck Yeager on the fortieth anniversary of the breaking
of the sound barrier. He said he would like to have Ellie
and me there as guests of the Marshall University Foundation. He was eager to get Chuck's close friends to come,
and mentioned the names of others who would be there.
We accepted and later learned that we would also be
attending a ceremony to unveil a statue of Chuck at
Hamlin High School in his hometown of Hamlin.

Chuck flew to Wright Patterson AFB, Ohio, in a Nevada
Air National Guard F-4 for some business with the Air

Force. On the morning of October 14 he flew the F-4 from Wright Patterson to Hamlin and made several passes over his old hometown. This was no surprise to the people of Hamlin, long since accustomed to the idea that anyone doing aerobatics over the town was bound to be Yeager. However, on that particular day, one of the teachers at Hamlin Elementary rang the fire bell so that the children could legally be outside to watch the noisy and exciting flyovers. Chuck then flew back to Ohio but returned about noon in a Marine Corps AV8B Harrier II jet fighter, which is capable of hovering or vertical flight. He flew over Huntington and Hamlin again and then landed at Tri-State Airport near Huntington.

After lunch with Marshall University people and friends, Chuck was flown in a helicopter to Hamlin for the statue ceremony while we drove over with the other participants.

I hadn't been in Hamlin since the late '40s, when Ellie and I drove there to visit Chuck, Glennis, and Chuck's family. It hasn't really changed that much. The road is still narrow and winding, following the bottom of the hollow between two ridges. There are a couple of ninety-degree turns in the road, and that's where Hamlin is located.

There were lots of welcome signs out and many, many people in the streets. People from all over, certainly many more than the population of Hamlin could produce. Chuck insisted that Ellie and I sit up on the speaker's platform. The Governor of West Virginia, Arch Moore, was there— members of Chuck's family, Hal and Pansy, Marshall University and local school officials, and the sculptor, Jim Lykins. Ellie and I were in the second row of the speaker's stand and had an excellent view of everything.

There were lots and lots of young people there. The

entire school yard was jam-packed with people. They even had to temporarily close the main road through town to accommodate everyone. Yet, even seated on the speaker's platform, there was a hometown feeling in the crowd as though this were a kind of extended family celebration for a son of whom they were particularly proud.

The youngest children crowded in the closest and were actually leaning on the front of the platform right near Chuck's feet. As I listened to Chuck's moving response to the Governor's short speech, I was watching the kids. There was one particular boy right in front who was looking up with absolute adoration. He appeared to be about nine years old and I noticed that a couple of times he even started the applause in response to Chuck's remarks. After the unveiling of the statue, just about everybody tried to swarm up onto the stage seeking autographs from Chuck. But later Chuck told me that this one boy grabbed his leg and asked Chuck to hold him. Chuck picked the kid up and as he was giving him a big hug the boy pressed his head on Chuck's shoulder, clinging like a limpet.

Chuck is not one to ever show much emotion or enthusiasm for these kinds of affairs. He's been to so many ceremonies that he takes them all pretty much in stride. But he was truly moved by this outpouring of admiration from the people of his hometown, most of them so young they knew him only by reputation. The Yeagers have been a Hamlin family for a long time and the feeling was very personal and very real. And Chuck was clearly having a great time. . . .

Which brings up a point. I think "fun" is the most important word in Chuck's vocabulary. Next to "press on" anyway. His attitude has always been: "If something's not fun, why do it?" What he does, really, is manage to *make* fun from just about any situation he encounters. I went to our Fighter Group reunion not long ago, and after all these years, I saw something there that summed up Chuck Yeager pretty neatly. There was this former Red Cross girl who was passing around a scrapbook that had pictures of us in wartime England. One in particular caught my eye because it was of a bunch of pilots standing on a beach amidst those dragon-toothed anti–invasion devices that they had embedded along the shore. Everyone was in uniform except for one guy. There, lying out on the sand in front of the others—and wearing swimming trunks and a big smile—was my friend Yeager. Now, it would never have occurred to me, in the middle of the daily life-and-death struggle of a major war, to go swimming. But apparently, it had occurred to Chuck, and he'd even managed somehow to get himself a pair of trunks.

So while "fun" may be altogether too limited a word to define the many different kinds of feelings Chuck gets from his all-out approach to living—all the way from the tough-won serenity of the Sierras to the high of aerial combat—it is the word he would use in his thinking; it's how he'd define whether or not a thing was worth doing, or a person worth knowing.

THE YEAGER SCHOLARSHIP PROGRAM

I was never all that good a student, so I guess it's kind of ironic that both the old high school and Marshall University should decide to honor me—the first with a life-size statue and the second with a scholarship fund.

I'm not one for formal occasions, maybe because I've had to attend more than my fair share, but that ceremony in Hamlin was right up my alley—a bunch of good people, of all ages, most of whom knew each other (and a good many probably related one way or another) getting together to celebrate and have some fun. That kid who came up to me, maybe someday he'll be a flier—maybe not. But whatever it is he ends up doing, I hope he got the message—go all out for it, balls-out as we say, and have a damn fine time doing it.

The other half of that memorable October 14 was spent with the Marshall University people. They have all the memorabilia Glennis was sorting and packing a while back and have set up a foundation, formally titled "The Marshall University Society of Yeager Scholars." Their motto is "Only the Best." Joe Hunnicutt is the leading light behind all this.

At a black-tie dinner that evening we met the first group of twenty students selected for the program—an impressive bunch. They all got full scholarships, board, and spending money for the four-year term. Special courses will be required of them (such as the Art of Negotiation) in addition to the regular curriculum they choose. They will be provided with meaningful summer jobs with major U.S. industries. Furthermore, there will be opportunities for foreign travel in the summer, and even for jobs abroad so that they can get to rub noses with other cultures, meet students like themselves, and establish personal relationships that may help in later years. Each year Marshall hopes to recruit twenty students from all over the nation to mold into world-class citizens. As far as I'm concerned, they couldn't have picked a better objective.

If I'm not one for formal occasions, I'm even less one for looking back. On the other hand, that's what a book is all about, and if that's the job, you do it—and get as much of a bang out of it as you can. What I call "the hero business" is something I've gotten used to—hell, might as well admit I enjoy it, at least in my hometown—but for a very long time I myself was just simply amazed by all the attention I was getting for the X-1 flight. The way I viewed things back then, my greatest achievement was becoming a double ace with my P-51 Mustang in World War II. I'd been raised to believe that you could do nothing more important than to fight for your country. But the public saw things differently during the late '40s and '50s. In that era, when jet propulsion was something new and exotic, and radically redesigned airplanes were being rolled out of hangars every day, there was no occupation more glamorous than test pilot.

We research fliers used to laugh among ourselves and say we were on the "foreskin of technology." But the public took us very seriously. And because I had the luck to break the sound barrier, I suppose I was the ultimate version of this twentieth-century cowboy. It didn't matter that one of the things I'd proved in the X-1 was that there was really no sky demon who pulled apart your airplane if it dared to exceed Mach 1, the way some scientists had feared. An entirely new thing had been done and *Time* magazine put me on its cover—we have the original painting hanging in our hallway.

But there's famous and there's *famous*, I've learned. Throughout the '50s and '60s, and right up until I retired in '75, I gave a steady stream of speeches and interviews on behalf of the Air Force. I didn't get mobbed in restaurants, or swarmed after by bobby-soxers, but people knew who I was. Cards and letters came in constantly. And if there was something concerning aviation in the news, it wasn't unusual for a reporter to track me down and ask for a comment.

But then in 1980, five years after I retired from the Air Force as a brigadier general, all hell broke loose in terms of phones ringing and people writing in with every imaginable kind of proposition. Suddenly I couldn't go to the local donut shop to get a cup of coffee without someone asking for an autograph. "I thought the public is supposed to have a short memory," I said to Glennis one day when we had two people on hold and a reporter banging on the door. "What the hell's going on?"

Actually, the answer to that question was obvious. Tom Wolfe had published his book, *The Right Stuff*, the book had led to a movie on which I served as technical advisor, the movie led to TV commercials, and in the meantime I had worked with Leo Janos on my own first book, which, I'm happy to say, racked up phenomenal sales and made me a household name in the kind of households that don't know the X-1 from a B-22.

But the real reason I was suddenly a hot commodity went beyond all the exposure I was getting. All that publicity about me would have fallen on deaf ears if the American public hadn't been hungry for heroes. All through the '70s and '80s, politically this country had been taking a beating. America needed a hero to hug, and I was it. Well, okay.

To hear yourself described that way is very humbling, and I've no idea if I really fit the bill. All I can tell you is that I'm a fighter pilot and a research flier, a hunter and a fisherman. What I like I enjoy immensely, and what I don't like I don't bother with at all. I don't waste time

245

regretting any down times and stretches in life. I never tie myself into knots trying to see both sides of every argument.

I can't really take credit for being that way, because it's the only way I know. I also know that when things are going great, goddamn, you better keep your eyes open, because the pendulum swings both ways in life. When things are going really well, I begin to watch. It's just like with airplanes: with everything going perfectly, that's when the good ol' sixth sense goes into operation so the whole thing doesn't blow up in your face. That's part of the mechanics of being a good pilot, a good hunter, a good fisherman—you know if it's a beautiful day, *enjoy* it. Chances are you'll get hailed on or snowed on the next day.

So fame makes you kind of cautious, a bit anxious to guard your privacy. You also realize how lucky you are that you're still living to see the recognition—and the problems that it generates. It takes a while to learn, but again, that's your job, so you might as well do as well as you can and enjoy the whole thing. And I can understand the need to have heroes. I've looked up to people, too, even if almost no one else has ever heard of them. Grandpa Yeager; my uncle Richard who was killed in World War I; and Albert Yeager, my dad: they were my heroes. These were mountain men who could build a barn, shoot a bear, and fix the engine on their pickup trucks—all without a lick of help. They understood the natural world and how it worked and had a deep respect for nature. Drop them deep in the woods and they'd not only live to tell about it, they'd survive in style. They were self-sufficient—as far from fame and fortune as human beings can be. But because they knew they could handle themselves in any

LEE COUNTY LIBRARY
107 Hawkins Ave.
Sanford, NC 27330

246

situation, they were rich in two very important things: self-confidence and peace of mind.

Grandpa Yeager, Uncle Richard, and Dad were men who lived the lives they wanted to lead, no matter what. I thought of them after I was shot down over France, as I made my way back to our base in England, arriving more tanned and fit than the guys who'd never stopped flying. And I still often think of those three West Virginia men who died without much in the way of worldly possessions but who, for me, still personify success because they truly knew how to *live*. That's what it's all about. So enough looking back—press on.